SAILING

Start Windsurfing Right!

The national standard of quality instruction for anyone learning how to windsurf

A proven system for becoming a confident, safe sailor… fast!

Based on original text by James Coutts

SECOND EDITION

This book is dedicated

to the "unsung" Instructors

and Instructor Trainers who have

given their best in making our

sport a safe and enjoyable

learning experience.

ISBN 978-1-882502-96-7

Second Edition, copyright © 2001 by the United States Sailing Association
Second Printing, 2010

United States Sailing Association
15 Maritime Drive, P.O. Box 1260
Portsmouth, RI 02871

401 683-0800
Fax: 401 683-0840

info@ussailing.org
www.ussailing.org

Cover photographs: Susie Dornellas, Calema Windsurfing, Merrit Island, Florida

Illustrations are from the first edition of *Start Windsurfing Right!* © 1991
and by Eleanor Boober: pages 16, 22, 23, 24, 26, 27, 42, 43, 51, 52, 53,
54, 55, 56, 62, 63 (bottom left), 64, 69, 77 (bottom left), 83, 84, 113

Photographs:
Tinho and Susie Dornellas: page 25 and 121
Mercedes-Benz USA, LLC: page 139
Naish, a Division of Nalu Kai, Inc.: page 3
NeilPryde: page 136
Pam Benjamin: pages 11, 26, 27, 39, 40, 41, 51, 134, and 138

Special thanks for their help with sails and equipment to
Island Sports, Middletown, Rhode Island, and
Adventure Sports, Inc., Miami, Florida

Printed in the United States of America

Foreword

© Darrell Wong

Welcome to one of the greatest sports in the world, and prepare to get hooked. Windsurfing is incredibly addictive. Combining the best aspects of sailing, skiing, surfing, and flying, it's free, it's fast, it's exciting, and if you get started right — it's also easy to learn. After 26 years of windsurfing nearly every day, I still get a rush when I'm out on the water.

I got started as a kid, when the sport was in its very early stages of development. The sails were big and heavy, booms made of wood and the boards heavy and unstable. The system of teaching was also mostly trial and error. It took me days before I could get from point A to point B and back again. You are a lot luckier than I was. Today, windsurfing equipment is highly developed, making getting started a lot easier—and the possibilities from there are almost endless. The process of teaching windsurfing has also developed into an advanced art, to the point where new sailors can learn in a flash (and maybe a splash or two).

Remember, getting started right means less time splashing, and more time sailing. It also means you'll advance your windsurfing skills faster and farther. And that's the most fun of all.

Aloha, and good sailing!

Robbie Naish

For the last 26 years, Robby Naish has been the world's premier windsurfer, winning the Windsurfer World Championship in '76, '77, '78, and '79. After turning pro, he won the Professional World Championship in '83, '84, '85, '86 and '87. In 1988 he won the Wave Performance World Championship. Robby maintains a hectic schedule, traveling extensively to promote Naish Sails and Kites, and making personal appearances on behalf of his various sponsors. He still competes in selected windsurfing world cup events and spends as much time kiteboarding as he can. He placed second in the recent "KING OF THE AIR" competition on Maui. Born in La Jolla, California, he lives in Hawaii, his favorite sailing grounds.

Acknowledgments

Windsurfing is exhilarating. If you have watched someone glide across the water with a sail filled with invisible power, you have probably been amazed. The formula for successful windsurfing is contained in this publication. Learning this exhilarating sport will be easy and fun thanks to a dedicated group of professional instructors who have committed to developing a system of getting people started in windsurfing the right way.

The United States Sailing Association (US SAILING) is proud to present the new, revised edition of *Start Windsurfing Right!*, the true national standard of windsurfing instruction.

However, the main people who make the system work are the certified Instructors and the US SAILING Instructor Trainers. Their high standards and dedication to clear and effective teaching, along with their commitment to safety are very important to the quality of windsurfing in this country.

In particular, US SAILING would like to commend the never-ending support and contributions of Beth Powell, Master Instructor Trainer (Cocoa Beach, Florida) and Tinho Dornellas, Master Instructor Trainer (Merritt Island, Florida) for continuing to make this system the best in the world. To add to the value of this book are the contributions of Ann Adair (Merritt Island, Florida), Andy Brandt (Alamonte Springs, Florida), Jackie Butzen (Chicago, Illinois), Sande "PC" Dickinson (Enumclaw, Washington), Petra Kanz (Kill Devil Hills, North Carolina), James Coutts (Scotland), and Pam Benjamin, US SAILING staff member. Special thanks to Ian Parker (Bristol, Rhode Island), Bill Barnes (Portsmouth, Rhode Island), and Holly Macpherson (Hood River, Oregon), former Executive Director of US Windsurfing. Holly has provided the belief and support in this program since its inception, and has been a great supporter.

Special thanks to all of you, for without you this publication would not be possible.

Contents

Chapter 4 – Understanding Wind

Chapter 5 – How a Sail Works

Chapter 6 – Rigging & De-Rigging

Chapter 7 – Your First Sail

Chapter 14 – Beyond the Basics

Appendix

Introduction

The United States Sailing Association (US SAILING) is our nation's governing body for the sport of sailing. US SAILING provides unprecedented support for American sailors at all levels of sailing on boards and sailboats. Its primary objective is to provide an effective standard of quality instruction for all people learning to sail. The US SAILING program for windsurfing includes *Start Windsurfing Right!*, a program of student certification and an extensive educational and training program for instructors themselves. It is one of the most highly developed and effective national training systems for students and sailing instructors in the world.

This program is conducted at a professional level to ensure a high degree of continuity and success for its students. Our hope is that you will become a safe and successful sailor who will enjoy the unique thrill and rewards of windsurfing!

The national instructional method for instructors and students supported by US SAILING is the Standards for Training with Accelerated Results Method. This learning and teaching process is designed to develop safe, responsible and confident sailors who meet specific performance and knowledge standards. (See *Certificate Record – Parts 1 and 2* in the back of this book for the basic windsurfing standards.)

How to Use This Resource Book

Start Windsurfing Right! is intended as a supplement to your first lessons, rather than as a substitute for them. It was created to help build your enthusiasm and make your introduction to the fantastic sport of windsurfing a positive experience that you will carry far into the future. Use it as a tool to accelerate your learning curve and clarify your understanding of the principles and techniques of windsurfing.

This book, in conjunction with qualified instruction, places the emphasis on getting on the water quickly and learning windsurfing skills "by doing." This will make your learning experience more exciting and immediately satisfying.

Start Windsurfing Right! has been written and designed for quick understanding and easy access.

- On each spread is a description of the topic discussed.

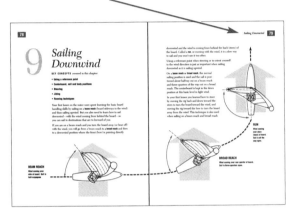

- Text has been kept concise and to the point, with key terms in bold for clarity and easy location.

- Diagrams and text are designed to work independently as well as together.

To use the book most effectively, we encourage you to follow these steps:

1. Be committed and enthusiastic about learning.

2. Learn to sail with a qualified school and instructor.

3. Read each chapter thoroughly.

4. Examine each of the illustrations. They have been carefully designed to help you visualize concepts and procedures clearly and simply.

5. Practice each sailing maneuver on shore and then on-the-water.

6. Review each chapter and be sure you understand it before moving on to the next one.

Remember, your own rate of learning may be different from other students based on a number of factors, the most important being your commitment to becoming a good sailor. Also remember that a good sailor—even a great one—never stops learning.

What Makes Windsurfing Special?

Whether you're young or old, a marathon runner or sedentary couch potato, you can enter the exciting world of windsurfing—a unique combination of sailing and surfing introduced in 1968 by Southern Californians Hoyle Schweitzer and Jim Drake. Described as a "free-sail system," windsurfing combines a sailor and a minimal amount of equipment to produce one of the most enjoyable, physically exhilarating, and totally refreshing recreational experiences available.

The essential equipment is remarkably simple: a board (with a skeg and centerboard), and a rig consisting of a mast with a universal joint, a boom, and a sail. The rig is free to move in any direction (no rigging restricts its movement) and is also used to steer the board (a rudder is not used)—hence the term "free-sail."

Windsurfing is low-cost and low-maintenance. All you need is water, wind and a beach and you're in business! You can also carry a board and rig on the roof of your car with ease. Windsurfing is a notable exception to the expression, "You can't take it with you."

Young or old, most sailors find that formal instruction is the fastest, safest and most fun method of learning.

Selecting a School

Teaching yourself windsurfing can be a lengthy, frustrating, and even hazardous undertaking. Most sailors find that formal instruction is the fastest, safest and most fun method of learning. Participation in a US SAILING-approved instructional program ensures that you start out on the right foot. There are many such schools throughout the country.

When selecting a school or course you should look for the following:

1. A US SAILING-approved school.

2. US SAILING-certified instructors. (Ask to see their current certificates.)

3. Stable sailboards with training sails. (See "Equipment Selection," pages 133-136 in the *Appendix,* for additional information.)

4. A "dry land" simulator, which allows the board to rotate as you move the sail. It is used to practice windsurfing techniques on land before doing them on the water.

5. Courses offering US SAILING Level 1 Windsurfing Certification, which is issued upon successful completion of the course. This qualification is recognized and accepted worldwide by member countries of the International Sailing Schools Association.

Start Windsurfing Right! was designed to be used in conjunction with a US SAILING-approved course of instruction.

A Prerequisite — Swimming

There is one basic skill which you must have mastered before learning to sail a board—that is swimming. US SAILING and the American Red Cross require that students be able to swim at least 25 yards and tread water while fully clothed for at least five minutes in deep water (more than six feet deep), without assistance or the use of a life jacket. There are many excellent swimming courses available through the American Red Cross and your local YMCA and YWCA.

Welcome to the sport of windsurfing!

Start Windsurfing Right!

1 You as a Sailor

KEY CONCEPTS covered in this chapter:

- **Sailor's code**
- **Environmental awareness**
- **Self-reliant sailor**
- **Personal sailing gear**
- **Sun protection**
- **Warm-up exercises and stretching**

"First time windsurfing, right?"

There is an unwritten code among sailors which has been passed down through the centuries. It is based on courtesy, consideration, a respect for mother nature, a respect for fellow boaters, and coming to the assistance of those in trouble windsurfing.

There are common courtesies and specific "rules of the road" that allow everyone to share the water and maintain order at the same time. These range from the general "rule" that sailcraft (including windsurfers) have right-of-way over most powercraft to staying clear of swimming, scuba-diving and water skiing areas, and observing local laws and regulations. *Chapter 12 – Rules of the Road* covers some of these important rules.

Above all, good sailors exercise caution, consideration and common sense on the water. This attitude should be an important point of pride for **any** sailor.

As a sailor, you will discover that weather conditions play an important part in windsurfing and can change quickly on the water. A beautiful sunny day with a warm gentle sea breeze can rapidly turn cold with gusty winds. But you can anticipate and be prepared for these changes by developing an awareness of the environment around you.

Environmental awareness calls for continuous observation of wind, weather, sea, and current conditions, as well as your position relative to the shore and other watercraft. As you learn to understand and use these factors, you will become a safe and self-reliant sailor who will be able to sail confidently and safely in different weather conditions.

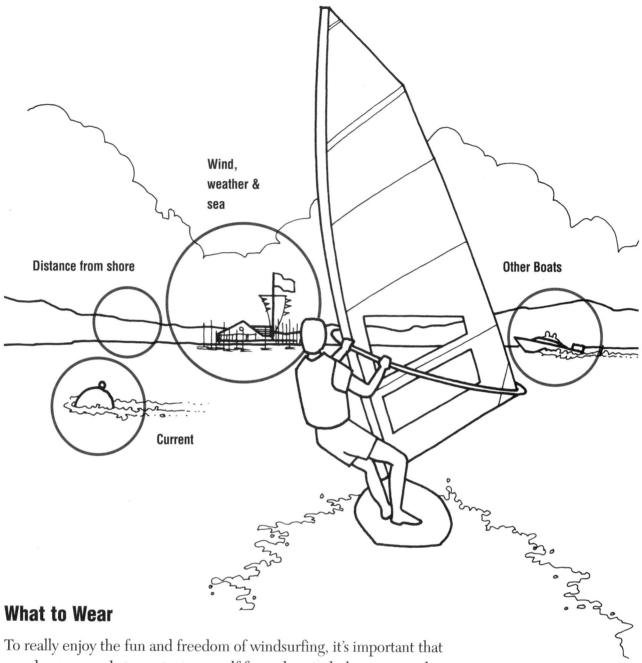

Wind, weather & sea

Distance from shore

Other Boats

Current

What to Wear

To really enjoy the fun and freedom of windsurfing, it's important that you dress properly to protect yourself from the wind, the water, and the sun. Your windsurfing school will provide the equipment you need, but you are responsible for wearing suitable clothes.

Windsurfing is a very active sport. Always wear clothing that will allow you to move easily and comfortably when bending, twisting, pulling, and pushing. A swimsuit or shorts with a light-colored shirt are fine for warm weather. But, if the water temperature is below 60 degrees or the combination of air and water is less than 120 degrees, a wetsuit or a drysuit should be worn. Local conditions and individual tolerances to cold may require wearing a wetsuit at higher temperatures.

HOT TIP!

If the water temperature is below 60 degrees or the combination of air and water is less than 120 degrees, a wetsuit or a drysuit should be worn.

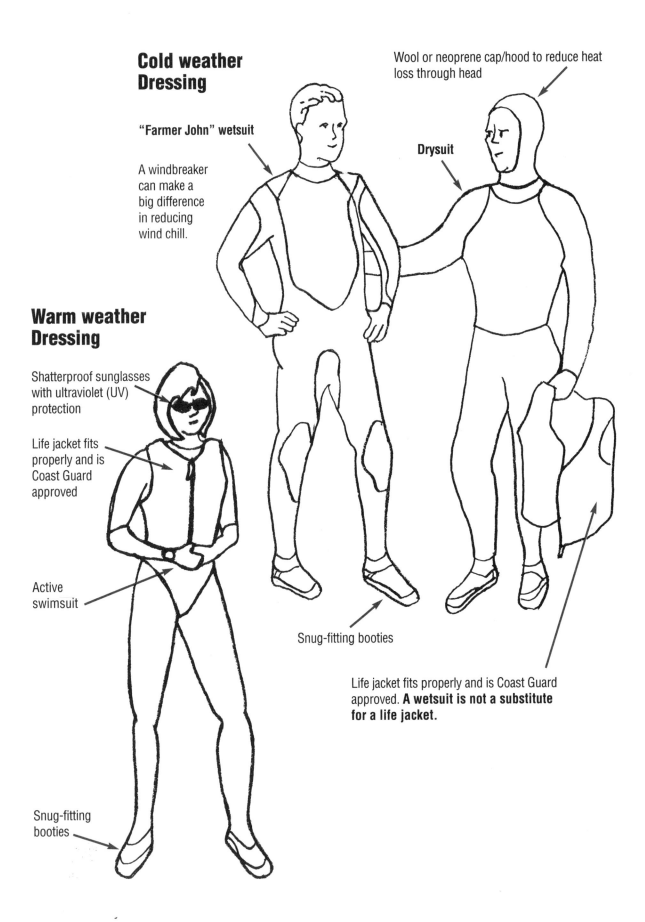

Cold weather Dressing

"Farmer John" wetsuit

A windbreaker can make a big difference in reducing wind chill.

Wool or neoprene cap/hood to reduce heat loss through head

Drysuit

Warm weather Dressing

Shatterproof sunglasses with ultraviolet (UV) protection

Life jacket fits properly and is Coast Guard approved

Active swimsuit

Snug-fitting booties

Snug-fitting booties

Life jacket fits properly and is Coast Guard approved. **A wetsuit is not a substitute for a life jacket.**

You should always wear snug-fitting, rubber-soled shoes for good traction on the board and to protect your feet when launching in shallow water. Lightweight sneakers or running shoes work well, but you may want to use a pair you can afford to get soaked! There are also special windsurfing boots or slippers which are comfortable and durable.

Jewelry, such as earrings, neck and ankle chains should not be worn.

Sun Protection

To protect yourself against the sun, wear a shirt, hat or visor, and sunglasses, and use a high-numbered sunscreen (such as a 15 Sun Protection Factor) on all exposed skin (non-oily, so it won't wash off). Lip balm protection is often overlooked and can save much discomfort. If you sunburn easily, wear a shirt with long sleeves and a high collar. And don't forget, even on cloudy days the sun's ultraviolet rays will penetrate the overcast.

You won't be having fun if you're freezing or frying, so **dress sensibly for the conditions!**

Warm Up!

You can increase your enjoyment of windsurfing by being physically fit. And windsurfing itself serves as the best form of strength and endurance conditioning, allowing you to improve your skill and fitness levels simultaneously.

Aerobic and anaerobic exercises, and warm-up and cool-down activities can also improve your general level of fitness and performance. Aerobic exercise, such as fast walking, tennis, and bicycling, increases cardiovascular fitness and endurance. Anaerobic exercise uses lifting or pulling to help improve muscular strength and tone. Weight lifting and certain types of flexing and stretching exercises are anaerobic.

As part of your warm-up and cool-down exercises, get into the habit of doing some **stretching exercises** before and after you sail. This improves flexibility.

Fitness

You can increase your enjoyment of windsurfing by being physically fit. Windsurfing itself serves as strength and endurance conditioning, allowing you to improve your skill and fitness levels simultaneously.

Safety & You

KEY CONCEPTS covered in this chapter:

- **Stay with the board**
- **Buddy system**
- **Life jackets (PFDs)**
- **Signaling for help**
- **Hypothermia**
- **Heat emergencies**
- **Safety code**

The most fundamental safety concept to learn and remember is **stay with the board**! If you get tired, or have an equipment failure, or the wind and weather become too rough to sail back, **never** leave your board to try to swim ashore—**always** stay with the board. Think of your board as a life raft. (Self-rescue techniques using your board are covered in *Chapter 6 – Rigging and De Rigging.*)

"James, I think you're taking this buddy thing a bit too far."

The Buddy System

Another important safety concept is to **always sail with a friend**. This is called the "buddy system." Besides keeping an eye on each other, you can also have more fun and learn more while sailing with a buddy. It gives you the opportunity to compare your board handling skills as you improve them.

Life Jackets

No matter how windy or calm it may be, US SAILING-approved schools and instructors require that you wear a life jacket. Also called a **PFD**, or Personal Flotation Device, such jackets or vests are essential for safe windsurfing. The modern PFD is light and comfortable to wear and far superior to the outdated and bulky capok filled version. There are many reasons for wearing a life jacket:

- It adds buoyancy to your body in the water
- It keeps your body warm
- It builds confidence when you are learning to sail.

Your life jacket should be Coast Guard approved. The notice of approval is always sewn or stamped on the vest. Choose a color of the PFD that is easily visible when you are on or in the water — yellow or orange are more visible than blue or white. An important accessory to your PFD is a whistle, which can be used to attract attention or help. They are easy to attach with a short length of line. Spend some time becoming familiar with your life jacket on land before using it on the water.

Signaling for Help

If you require assistance, you should use the **international distress signal** to attract attention and get assistance. To use this signal, raise and lower your outstretched arms with clenched fists above your head and down to your sides-slowly and repeatedly—while blowing the whistle attached to your life jacket. The sound of a whistle travels much farther and better than shouting. If you feel you need help, seek it immediately. Putting it off will only make matters worse. But remember, **always stay with your board—don't try to swim for shore!**

Use the international distress signal if you need assistance on the water.

Hypothermia and Heat Emergencies

It is vital that you dress properly for cold conditions. Cold air temperatures and/or cold water can cause a life-threatening condition called **hypothermia**. This occurs when the body's normal core temperature (98.6 degrees F) is lowered. To help prevent hypothermia, it is best to wear a wet or drysuit and a cap or hood to reduce heat loss.

Most sailors do not consider **heat emergencies** to be a threat while sailing. But on hot humid days—with or without a breeze—anyone can be affected by the heat. People who are especially susceptible to extreme heat are the very young, very old, chronically ill, overweight, those who work in hot places, and athletes. Heat emergencies include **heat stroke, heat exhaustion, or heat cramps**.

Drinking cold water at regular intervals before, during, and after you sail is the best defense for heat emergencies, along with cooling off in the water. Anyone sailing in hot weather (or in cold weather when wearing a wet or drysuit) should drink at least one pint of chilled water per hour while on the water. Wearing lightweight, light-colored clothing, a hat or visor, and sunglasses also helps prevent heat emergencies.

HOT TIP!

To prevent hypothermia: wear a wet or drysuit and a cap or hood to reduce heat loss.

To prevent heat emergencies: Drink water regularly, cool off in the water, and wear light-weight, light-colored clothing, a hat or visor, and sunglasses.

Hypothermia

SIGNALS

- Shivering
- Impaired judgement
- Dizziness
- Numbness
- Confusion
- Weakness
- Impaired vision
- Drowsiness

Physical symptoms
for hypothermia, heat stroke
and heat exhaustion may
vary, since age, body size,
and clothing will cause
individual differences.

TREATMENT

Medical assistance should be given to anyone with hypothermia.
Until medical assistance arrives, these steps should be taken:

- Move the person to a warm place and handle gently.
- Remove all wet clothing.
- Warm the body temperature gradually.
- Cover person with blankets or sleeping bags and insulate from cold.
- If the person is fully conscious and can swallow, give him or her something warm (not hot), such as warm broth or gelatin. If the person is not fully conscious, do not give any food or drinks.

The Stages of Hypothermia

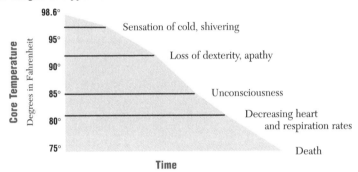

Heatstroke

SIGNALS

- Hot, red skin
- Constricted pupils
- Very high body temperature
- Skin will feel dry, unless the person is sweating from exertion

TREATMENT

Heat stroke is life threatening.

Anyone afflicted with heat stroke needs to be cooled down while a doctor or EMS technician is contacted immediately.

- Move person to cool environment.
- Cool person in cold bath or by wrapping wet towels or sheets around body.
- Contact a doctor or EMS (Emergency Medical Services) personnel.
- Do not give person anything to eat or drink.

Heat Exhaustion

SIGNALS

- Cool, pale, moist skin
- Heavy sweating
- Dilated pupils
- Headache
- Dizziness
- Nausea
- Vomiting

TREATMENT

Heat exhaustion is less dangerous than heat stroke.

First aid includes the following steps:

- Move person to cool environment.
- Care for shock by placing person on back with feet elevated 8-to-12 inches.
- Remove or loosen clothing.
- Apply wet towels or sheets.
- Give person half a glass of cool water every 15 minutes, if fully conscious and can tolerate it.

Safety in Mind

Being safety conscious at all times, both on and off the water, is an attitude you will develop with your instructor's help. It will pay off many times over in safe, fun, and relaxing sailing.

Safety encompasses many things: dressing properly, wearing a life jacket, being considerate and courteous toward other boaters, being observant, sailing by the "rules of the road," making sure your equipment is in good order, and checking existing weather conditions and any possible changes. Your instructor puts safety first and will pass his or her knowledge and philosophy of safety on to you. Listen to your instructor's advice and become familiar with the safety code.

An important part of enjoying the sport of windsurfing is a seamanlike attitude toward your equipment. Check your gear for wear or breakage **before you go out on the water.**

The Windsurfing Safety Code

1. Consider local weather and tidal forecasts.
2. Always advise someone of where you plan to sail and when you expect to return.
3. Wear clothing that suits the conditions.
4. Wear a U.S. Coast Guard-approved life jacket (PFD) with a whistle attached.
5. In hot, sunny, humid conditions, drink plenty of water.
6. Check your equipment for signs of damage or fatigue.
7. Sail with a buddy.
8. Do not sail in offshore winds.
9. Cold can kill. The first time you shiver, return to shore and warm up.
10. Always stay with your board—never try to swim ashore.

Before launching:

11. Double check your safety leash.
12. Be wary of dark clouds on the horizon—storms strike fast.
13. If in doubt, don't go out.
14. A smart sailor will always try to take the safest course of action before rescue is the only way out.

The Board

KEY CONCEPTS covered in this chapter:

- **The board**

- **Centerboard and skeg**

- **The rig**

As a beginning sailor, you should use a stable **recreational style** board, ranging in length from 9' to 12'6" with recommended volume of over 200L. This is the type favored by US SAILING-approved instructional programs. Generally, the board's outer shell is constructed of polyethylene or an ABS-type plastic material that is filled with foam to make your board unsinkable.

The front end (**bow**) of the board is pointed and the back end (**stern**) is blunt. The elongated hole or well through the center of the board holds the **centerboard**. On top of the board in front of the centerboard well is the attachment point (**mast step**) for the **mast**. The eye (**tow eye**) at the front end is used to tie the board to another object such as a dock or boat, or to attach a towrope.

On the underside near the back end of the board is a small underwater fin (**skeg**) that keeps the board tracking on line. The **centerboard** is a larger underwater fin that helps prevent the sailboard from slipping sideways. The centerboard rotates on a pivot within the centerboard well, which allows you to raise and lower it easily. Some older boards, however, are equipped with **daggerboards** that do not pivot, but are raised and lowered vertically.

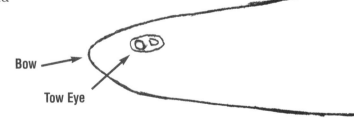

Bow

Tow Eye

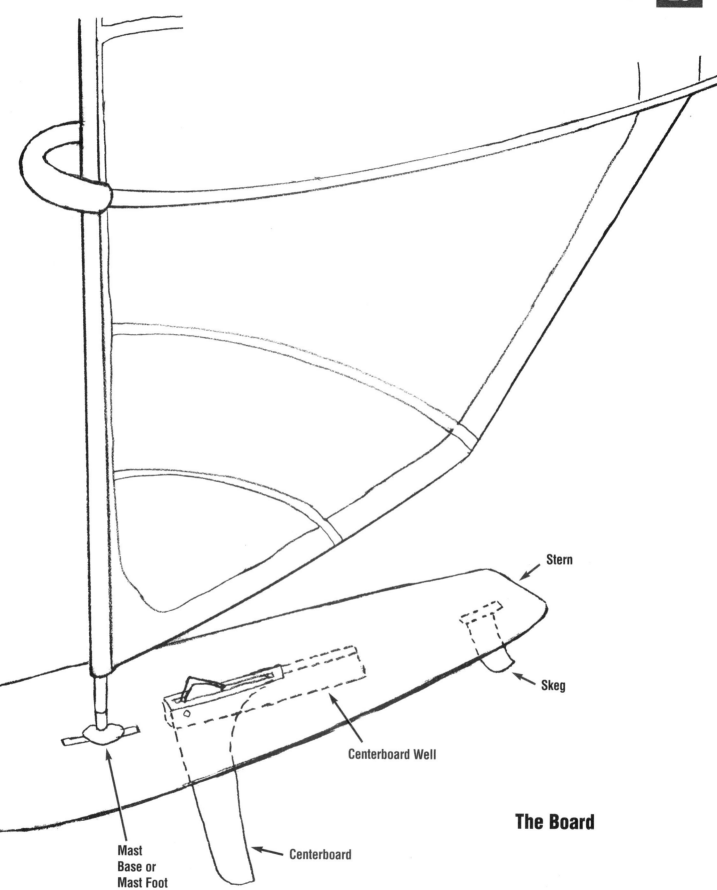

Stern

Skeg

Centerboard Well

The Board

Mast
Base or
Mast Foot

Centerboard

The Rig

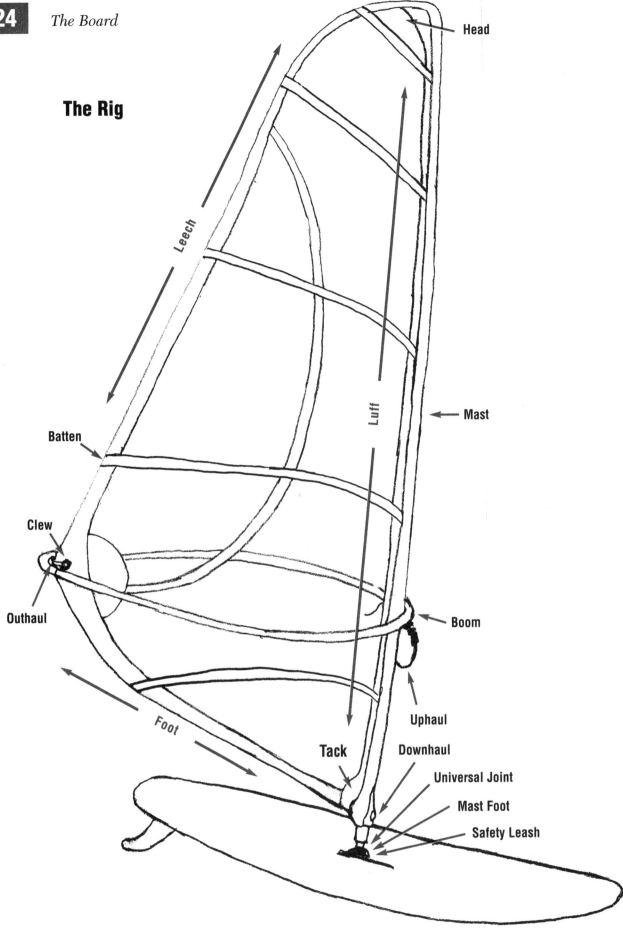

Head

Leech

Luff

Mast

Batten

Clew

Outhaul

Boom

Foot

Uphaul

Tack

Downhaul

Universal Joint

Mast Foot

Safety Leash

Parts of the Rig

The **sail** is basically triangular in shape. It has a sleeve running along its front edge (**luff**) into which the mast fits. Larger sails may have one or more narrow horizontal pockets (**batten pockets)** running across the sail. They hold **battens**, which are thin strips of flexible plastic or some other composite material that help support the sail's shape. School sails are smaller than full-sized recreational sails.

The **mast** is a hollow tube made of aluminum, fiber-glass, carbon fiber (or a combination of these) that is tapered to a smaller diameter at the top than at the bottom. The mast holds the sail up.

Fitted to the bottom of the **mast** is the mast foot with a **universal joint** that connects the mast to the board and allows the mast, boom, and sail to tilt and rotate in any direction.

Sometimes, a **mast extension** is added between the mast and mast foot to lengthen the mast to accommodate larger sails.

The rig consists of the mast, mast foot, boom, sail and sail control lines.

The **boom** is actually two curved tubes joined at the ends and is used to hold the sail out or "open." The front end of the boom is attached to the mast and the back end is connected to the back corner (**clew**) of the sail.

The **rig** consists of the mast, mast foot, boom, sail and sail control lines (*See opposite page*) assembled as a single unit.

The **uphaul** is a piece of thick rope (**line**) attached to the front end of the boom used to haul the rig up and out of the water. There is a short length of shock cord attached to the bottom of the uphaul with a clip to keep the uphaul close to the mast.

The **safety leash** or **strap** is a line that connects the rig and board, one end is attached to the bottom of the rig and the other end to the board. It prevents the board from drifting away from the rig if the mast foot fails or separates from the mast step.

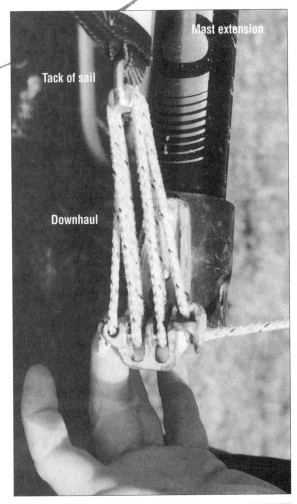

The **downhaul** attaches to and pulls the bottom corner (**tack**) of the sail down to the bottom of the mast. It also is used to adjust the tension on the front edge (**luff**) of the sail, which controls the curve, or shape of the sail.

Adjusting the downhaul (below).

The **mast foot** with a **universal joint** (above) that connects the mast to the board and allows the mast, boom, and sail to tilt and rotate in any direction.

A **clamp** (above left and right) attaches the front end of the boom to the mast.

The **outhaul** pulls the back corner (**clew**) of the sail out to the end of the boom and is also used to control the shape of the sail.

4 *Understanding Wind*

KEY CONCEPTS covered in this chapter:

- **Wind sensing**
- **Wind direction**
- **Puffs and lulls**
- **True wind**
- **Apparent wind**

"Okay, class, who can tell me which way the wind is blowing?"

Wind speed and direction never stay the same—they are constantly changing. While these changes are often small and subtle, they can be substantial. You will, with experience, develop a skill called **wind sensing** or **wind feel** which helps you detect the wind and anticipate its changes.

How can you tell the direction of the wind? The easiest way is to simply use your rig like a weather vane. Hold the rig upright and let it pivot freely. The front edge (**luff**) of the sail will point toward the wind (**upwind**) and the back edge will point away from the wind (**downwind**).

Other visual wind indicators are flags, smoke, and trees. Sometimes clouds can be used, since they often move in the same direction as surface wind.

As you become more experienced, you will also sense wind direction and speed by feeling the wind on your face and neck, and looking at the ripples or waves on the water. Ripples and waves are usually perpendicular to the wind.

Before your first sail, your instructor will show you how to determine wind direction and speed. By knowing where the wind is coming from, you will know the best way to prepare and carry the rig, launch, sail, and return to shore again.

WIND

Luff

If allowed to swing freely, the luff will always point toward the wind.

Visual Wind Indicators

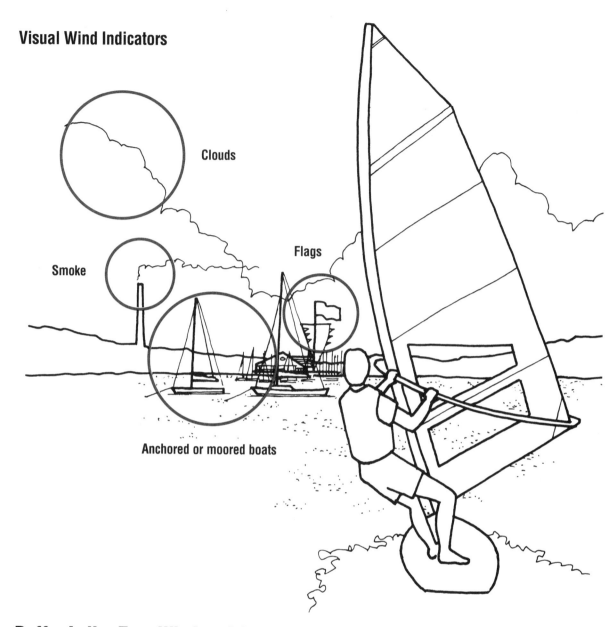

Clouds

Smoke

Flags

Anchored or moored boats

Puffs, Lulls, True Wind and Apparent Wind

Sudden changes in wind speed are called **puffs** or **lulls**. A **puff** is an increase in speed for a short duration, and a **lull** is a decrease in speed, sometimes called a "hole" in the wind. It is a rare day when the wind is truly steady. Most of the time, you will sail in and out of many puffs and lulls.

You can see and feel puffs and lulls. A puff usually makes the water surface look darker. A lull is a bit more difficult to see — usually lighter in color and smoother than the surrounding water. Get in the habit of always watching the water for puffs and lulls.

Visual wind indicators such as flags, smoke, and trees move in the same direction as surface wind.

Reading puffs on the water

Dark patch on water

In describing the speed or strength of the wind, the nautical term **knots**, is frequently used. One knot is about 20% more than one mile-per-hour (1 knot = 1.2 mph, or 10 knots = 12 mph).

When first learning to sail you may be confused by how the wind speed seems to almost disappear when you sail downwind (wind coming from behind the board) and increase again when you sail upwind (wind coming from ahead). To understand why this happens, you need to know the difference between **true wind** and **apparent wind**.

True wind is exactly that—the speed and direction of the wind that you feel when you are not moving. **Apparent wind** is a combination of the

Apparent Wind

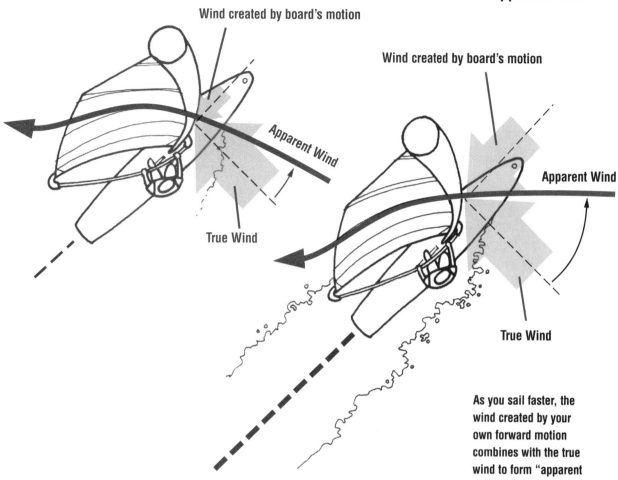

As you sail faster, the wind created by your own forward motion combines with the true wind to form "apparent wind" (right). The faster you move, the more the "apparent wind" direction moves toward the front of the board (left).

true wind and the wind created by your own motion. When you stick your hand out the window of a moving car, what you feel is apparent wind—wind created by the motion of the car in combination with the true wind that is blowing. The same phenomenon occurs—to a lesser extent—when your board moves. The faster your board is moving, the more apparent wind you create.

5 How a Sail Works

KEY CONCEPTS covered in this chapter:

- Lift
- Windward and leeward
- Steering
- Center of effort
- Center of lateral resistance

A sail works the same way for any type of sailing craft, whether it is an America's Cup yacht or your board. The sail uses the wind to generate forces, which push and/or pull your board forward.

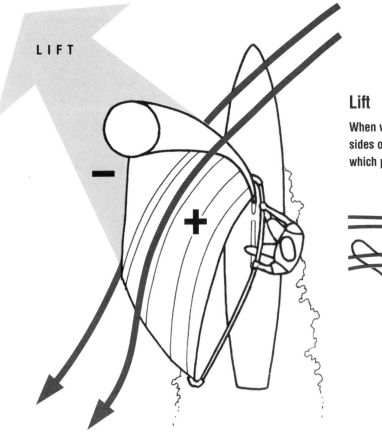

LIFT

Lift

When wind flows over both sides of a sail, "lift" is created, which pulls the board forward.

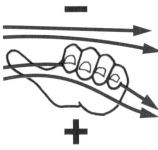

Windward and Leeward

It is important to understand the difference between these "push" and "pull" modes.

As the wind flows across **both** sides of a sail, it is re-directed by the sail's curved shape, creating lift. This pulls the board forward (and sideways, too, which is why a board has a centerboard). In this "**pull mode**," the sail functions similar to an airplane wing. As the wind splits to flow across the sail, there is more pressure on the side closest to the wind (**windward side**) than on the side away from the wind (**leeward side**), which results in a pulling or lifting action toward the leeward side. This particular theory of physics was discovered by Daniel Bernoulli in 1738 and is known as the **Bernoulli Principle**.

The sail can also generate force by simply blocking the wind. In this "**push mode**," the wind pushes against one side of the sail, moving the board in the same direction. Have you ever tried standing with your back to a very strong wind and felt it pushing you forward? The same

Two Big Words

The terms "windward" and "leeward," are important terms in your sailing vocabulary. You will hear them often.

- Windward refers to the side of the board or sail CLOSEST to the direction from which the wind is coming.

- Leeward is the side of the board or sail FARTHEST AWAY from the wind's direction.

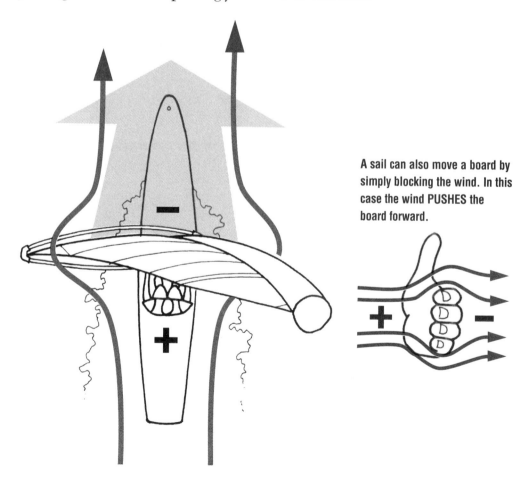

A sail can also move a board by simply blocking the wind. In this case the wind PUSHES the board forward.

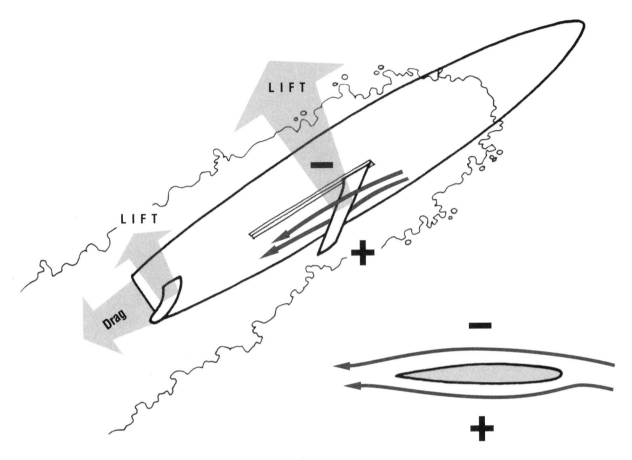

The centerboard and skeg also create lift which counteracts the sideways pull of the sail and keeps the board tracking straight.

thing happens on a board with the wind coming from behind you. The wind pushes your sailboard downwind rather than pulling it forward.

How a Board Moves Forward

There are more forces acting on a board than just lift from the sail. Remember that the lift created by the sail pulls the board not only forward, but also sideways (see page 35). To counteract this sideways pull, the board has underwater fins, the centerboard and skeg. They keep the board tracking forward by providing **lateral resistance** (sideways resistance), to the sideways pull of the sail.

Forward pull and push are also opposed by another, much smaller force —**drag**. Drag is the frictional resistance you and your board experience by moving forward through the air and water. After combining all these forces, lift from the sail, lateral resistance from the underwater fins and the drag on you and your board, the board moves forward with very little sideways motion.

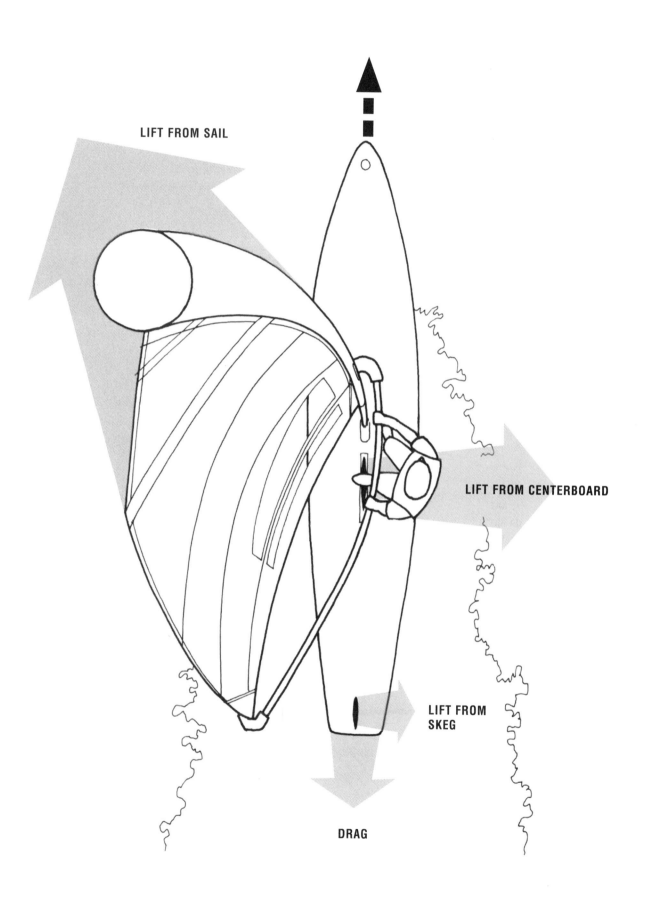

LIFT FROM SAIL

LIFT FROM CENTERBOARD

LIFT FROM SKEG

DRAG

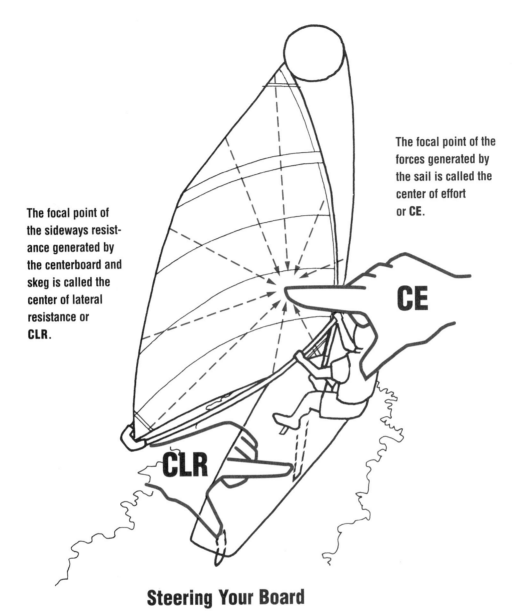

The focal point of the sideways resistance generated by the centerboard and skeg is called the center of lateral resistance or **CLR**.

The focal point of the forces generated by the sail is called the center of effort or **CE**.

CE

CLR

Steering Your Board

How do you steer your board? Simply by tilting the rig (mast, sail, and boom) toward the front or back of the board.

Why does this work? Because when you move the rig you move the focal point of all the forces acting on the sail (called the **Center of Effort**, or **CE**) in relation to the focal point of sideways resistance (called the **Center of Lateral Resistance**, or **CLR**) of the board. The CE is usually about one-third of the sail's width back from the mast, and the CLR is high up and near the middle of the centerboard.

The direction you tilt the rig to steer your board will not always be directly forward or backward. Sometimes—depending on your direction in relation to the wind—you will also move your rig to the side to steer.

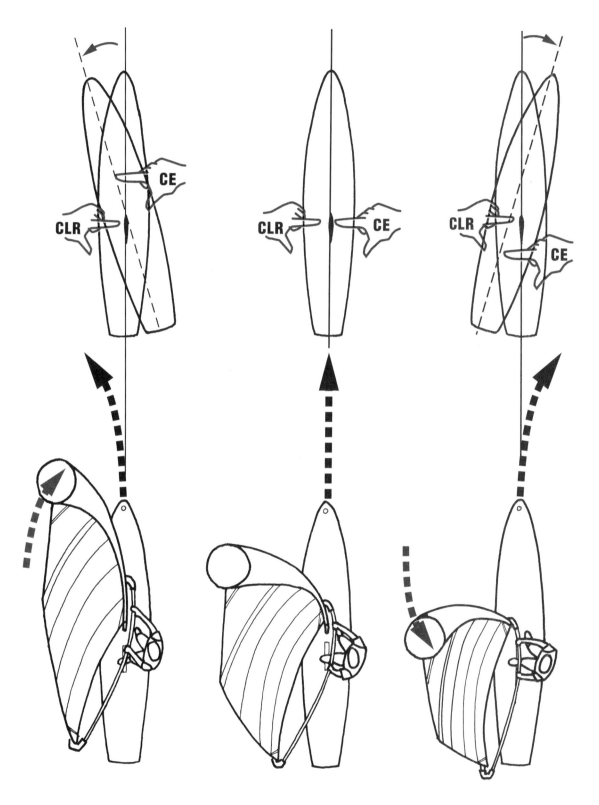

To turn **AWAY** from the wind, you move the rig **FORWARD** so the CE is **FORWARD** of the CLR.

To sail straight, you hold the rig so the CE and CLR line up.

To turn **TOWARD** the wind, you move the rig back so the CE is back (AFT) of the CLR.

6 Rigging & De-Rigging

KEY CONCEPTS covered in this chapter:

- **Back-to-wind position**
- **Rigging the sail**
- **Mast-to-wind position**
- **Carrying the rig**
- **De-rigging to self-rescue**
- **De-rigging for storage**

Although different brands of boards have different rig features, the basic rigging principles are the same for all. After a few times, you will be able to rig and de-rig with no help from your instructor. With a little practice, your rigging time will only be five-to-ten minutes.

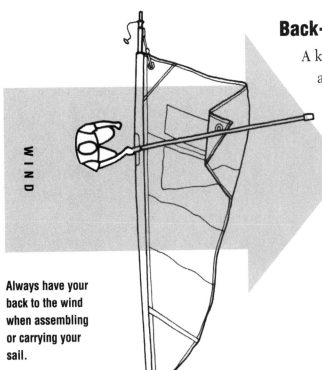

WIND

Always have your back to the wind when assembling or carrying your sail.

Back-to-Wind Position

A key concept when assembling and lifting the rig (mast, boom, and sail) is to **keep your back to the wind**. With your back to the wind, the sail will blow away from (not on top of) you as you unfold it, slide the mast into the sleeve, fit the mast foot, fasten the downhaul, and lift the rig upright.

The Rigging Sequence

1 Unfold sail, then slide mast into sleeve along forward edge (luff) of sail.

2 Slip mast foot into bottom of mast, then pass downhaul through hole in tack (bottom corner) of sail and into cleat. Tighten downhaul until there are no wrinkles on sleeve of sail.

3 With back-to-wind, stand mast upright and locate the point on mast that is level with your shoulders (where the boom connects), then lay mast down.

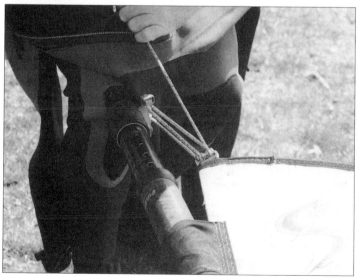

4 Slip boom over mast then secure boom to mast with clamp at shoulder height (the mast-to-boom connection should be firm and tight).

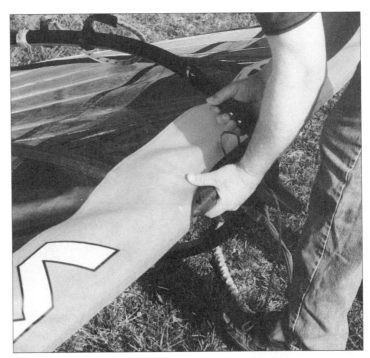

5 Attach shock cord at end of uphaul to down-haul using loop or clip on shock cord.

5 Pass outhaul through grommet in clew (back corner) of sail, through end of boom and into cleat; tighten and hitch off.

6 With back-to-wind, stand rig upright and let sail flag downwind so your instructor can check the tuning of the rig and height of boom, then lay rig down so mast is lengthwise across the wind. Battens should be tightened after the down-haul and outhaul have been tensioned.

Note: Many battens are tapered. The tapered end goes in the sail first.

Clew

Mast

Carrying Your Rig

Once you have finished the rigging sequence, the trick is to safely carry your rig to your board. In most instances, you have left your board near the water's edge and done the rigging operation a little farther up the beach.

The key is to lift and carry the rig so that the length of the mast is across the wind, the front end of the boom is pointing into the wind, and the sail is to leeward (downwind). This is called the **mast-to-wind position**.

Why is the mast-to-wind position so important? If you carry the rig any other way, it can blow out of your hands and go flying across the beach or parking lot. For the same reason, whenever you leave your rig unattended, make sure it is lying on the ground in the mast-to-wind position.

Mast-to-Wind Position

Whether getting ready to carry your rig or leaving it unattended, make sure it is lying in the mast-to-wind position.

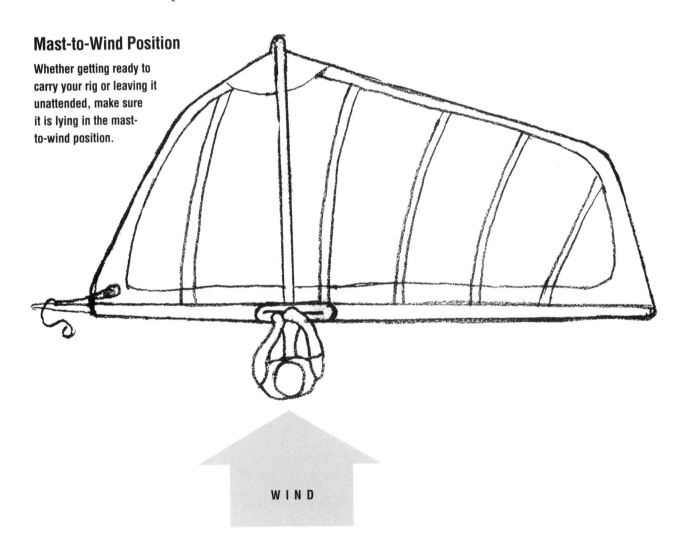

WIND

Lifting Sequence

Your instructor will demonstrate the best way to lift and carry your rig, but these are the basic steps to follow:

1 First, determine the wind direction and make sure the rig is in the mast-to-wind position. With your back-to-wind, grab the mast above the boom with one hand and the wide part of the boom with the other hand and lift the sail so the mast rests on your hip.

2 Move under the sail until you can grab the boom two feet from the mast, then raise the rig above your head, remembering to keep the mast lengthwise across the wind. If you want to turn, simply pivot your body beneath the rig, but keep the mast facing across the wind.

3 **POWER LIFT**
In gusty or high-wind conditions, rotating the mast foot slightly toward the wind will make it easier to control the rig.

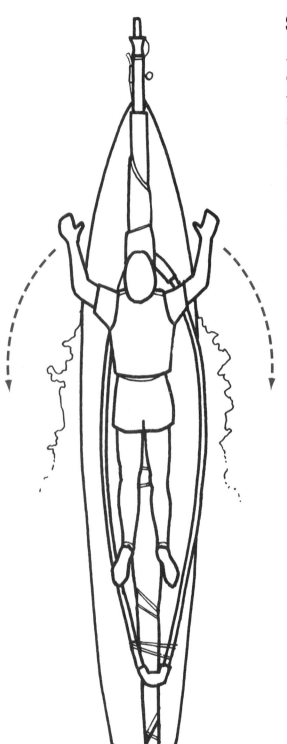

Self-Rescue

After you have assembled your rig and connected it to the board, your instructor will have you practice de-rigging to the **self-rescue position**, and then rigging up from this position. Self-rescue involves rolling up your sail, lashing the mast, sail, and boom together on top of your board and paddling back to shore.

You should only de-rig to the self-rescue position when you are confident that you can paddle to safety—either ashore or to an anchored boat or float. You should paddle directly against the wind only when there is no other alternative. It is best to look across the wind or downwind for a boat, island, sand bar, or buoy and paddle to a position that is upwind of it (*See page 49*).

De-Rigging for Self-Rescue:

Sequence for light winds and short distances:

1 **Leave sail rigged** and mast attached to board.

2 **Swing rig** across back of board and position boom on top of board so it holds sail out of water.

3 **Kneel** facing the bow with one leg each side of mast foot, then start paddling with both hands.

NOTE: This method should only be used when the wind is blowing less than 3 knots, the water is calm, and you have a short distance to paddle to shore or get away from a windless spot (such as trees or a harbor wall blocking the wind).

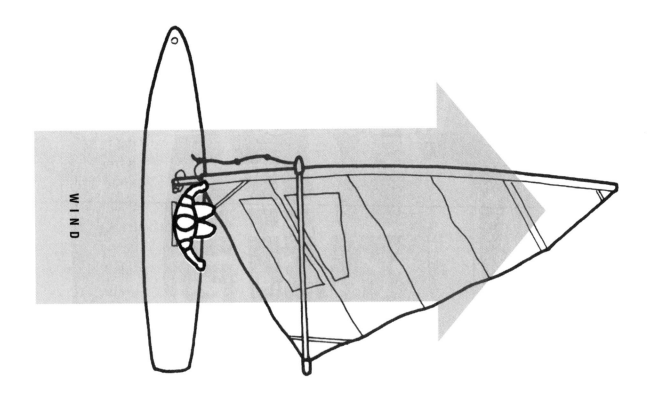

WIND

De-Rigging for Self-Rescue:

Sequence for light-to-moderate conditions:

Use **controlled drop method** (*See page 69*) to drop rig downwind with
mast facing the bow. Tell your buddy that you are going to de-rig
to self-rescue. Make sure centerboard is in the down position!
Sit down over centerboard, facing sideways with both legs
on same side between sail and board.

De-Rigging:

Sequence for Non-Swiveling Clamp on Boom

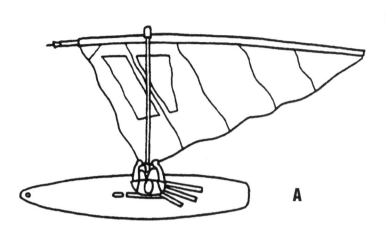

A

1 **Sit down** on board, legs in the water, facing toward the rig. Detach rig from board. Release uphaul. Remove all battens and sit on top of them (Figure A). Release outhaul completely. (Place battens alongside foot of sail and roll foot toward mast top.) As the sail is rolled up, the rig gets closer to the board. Allow the boom to go over and across the board (Figure B).

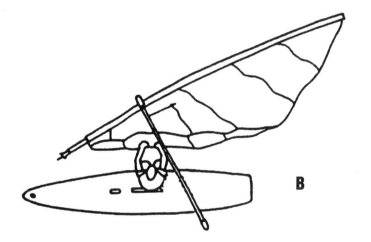

B

2 **Roll sail** tight until it goes along-side mast; mast now should be on your lap. Unclamp boom and pass uphaul around mast, so it holds the boom to the mast like an inhaul (Figure C).

3 **Wrap uphaul tightly in a wide spiral around bottom of mast and sail** in same direction as you rolled the sail, then secure clip at end of uphaul to shock cord. Move rig across your body and wrap outhaul around mast, sail and boom in same direction as you rolled sail. Pass end of outhaul through cleat at end of boom, and hitch off.

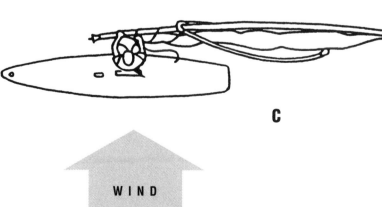

C

W I N D

4 **Rotate rig across board** between you and bow; make sure front end of boom is under mast. Then kneel over centerboard well, facing bow and rotate rig under your body, so mast foot is in front of and over the bow.

5 **Raise centerboard.** If it's a non-pivoting daggerboard, pull it out of the well and wedge it between mast and boom or tie it to rig to prevent loss. Lie down on top of rig, centering your body weight over centerboard well—you are now in the self-rescue position. Paddle toward shore using deep strokes. Breathe deeply between strokes.

SAFE & SOUND

You should not use self-rescue to compensate for your lack of sailing ability. Use your environmental awareness and wind sensing skills to help you determine whether the conditions are suitable for your level of experience.

A good rule of thumb is—if in doubt, don't go out.

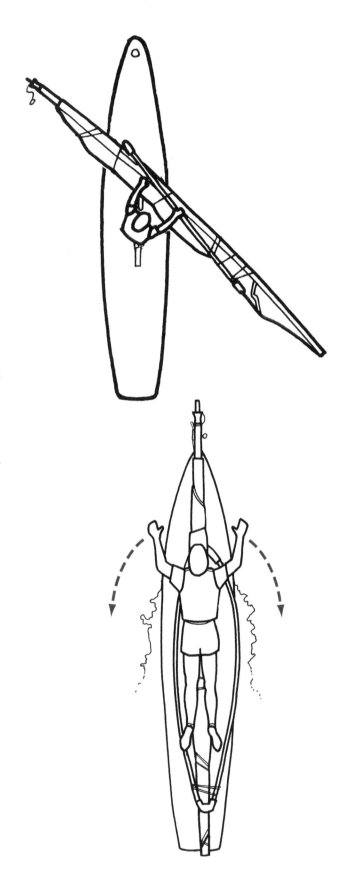

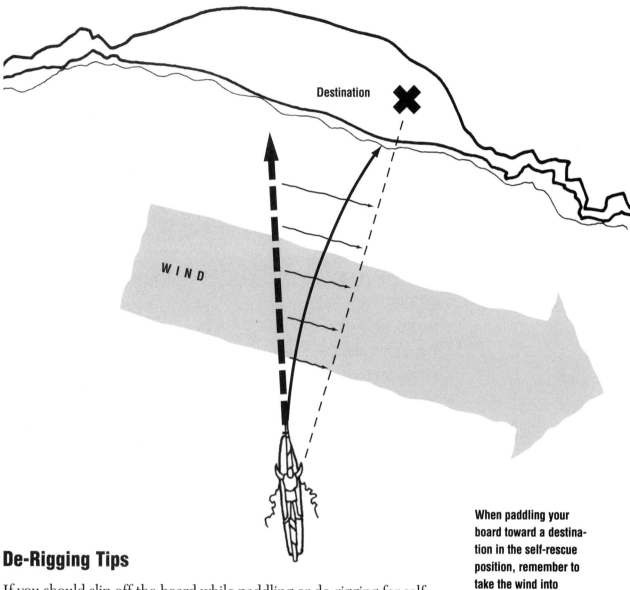

Destination

WIND

When paddling your board toward a destination in the self-rescue position, remember to take the wind into account

De-Rigging Tips

If you should slip off the board while paddling or de-rigging for self-rescue, get back onto the board first. Don't retrieve the rig until you are firmly back on the board. To make it easier to climb back onto the board, push the centerboard all the way down. When you are back on the board, follow the appropriate self-rescue procedure.

If you are unable to self-rescue and paddle to safety, use your rig as a sea anchor (or drogue) to decrease the drifting movement of the board as the wind blows you downwind. Drop the rig in the water on the downwind side of the board, and leave the mast foot attached to the board.

Stay with your board and conserve your energy!

As you gain experience and begin sailing in stronger winds, you should practice de-rigging and self-rescue. Know your limits, and be ready for the unexpected.

Your First Sail

KEY CONCEPTS covered in this chapter:

- **Safe Falling**
- **The land simulator**
- **Getting on the board**
- **Back-to-wind position**
- **Uphauling the rig**
- **Basic position**
- **Turning the board**
- **Starting and stopping**
- **Sailing position**
- **Controlling the sail**
- **Fail-safe position**
- **Trimming the sail**
- **Steering**
- **Dropping the rig**

Safe Falling

Falling is a healthy part of the learning process. Fall horizontally, if possible. Diving or jumping can result in jarring oneself on the bottom. Raise your hands crossed over your head when surfacing from a fall to avoid hitting your head on the board or the rig as it drops into the water.

Falling to leeward is accomplished by sheeting out quickly while bending knees, maintaining center of gravity over the board. If still overpowered, let go of the rig and bend knees further to a squatting position. If falling beside rig, push it away from body, keeping feet out from under mast.

Falling to windward is different in that you hold onto the rig to keep it from hitting your head and body while falling. Once in the water under the sail, place a hand on the mast and pull out and up to the surface toward the front of the board.

Land Simulator

Once you can rig and de-rig your board, you will be introduced to on-the-water skills on a **land simulator**. Your instructor will first demonstrate the basic positions and maneuvers on the simulator and then will work closely with you as you practice them. You will quickly gain a sense of balance and an understanding of the techniques needed to sail a board.

You will also develop a sense of "feel" for how things should be when they are done right. When something feels out of balance on the water, review the basic steps in your mind and remember how they felt on the simulator.

Land simulators help beginning sailors quickly gain an understanding of windsurfing balance and technique before they go out on the water.

Always get on the board from the side opposite the sail.

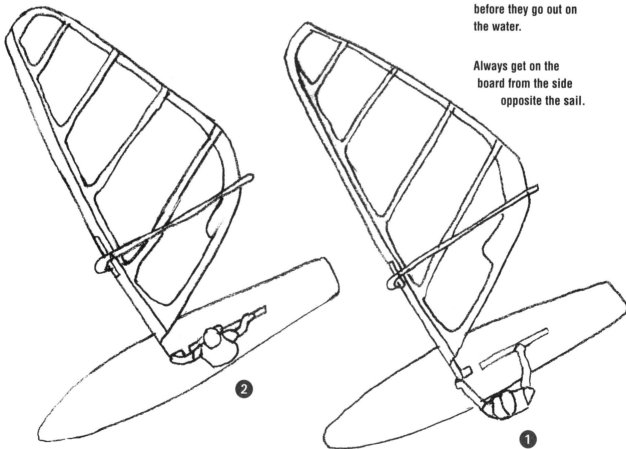

Getting on the Board

Always get on the board from the side opposite the sail. If you are in the water, pull yourself onto the board by grabbing the mast foot with your front hand and placing your back hand flat on the centerline of the board. Kneel on the board facing the sail. You are now ready to stand up and raise the rig from the water.

Uphauling Your Rig

Uphauling is hauling the rig up from the water. Start by determining which way the rig is lying in the water. Is it on the **downwind** or **upwind** side of the board?

Rig Downwind

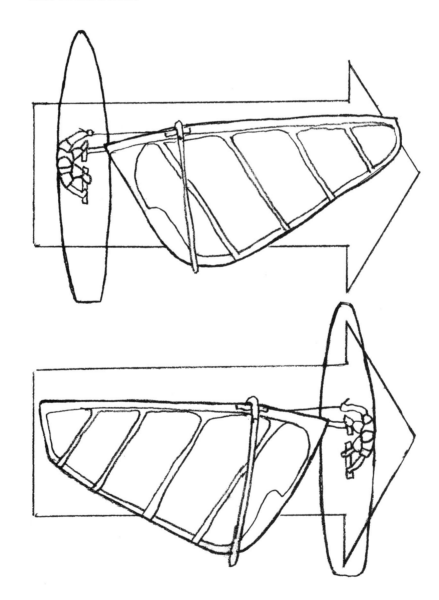

Rig Upwind

If the rig is downwind of the board, the top of the mast will point downwind and you will feel the wind on your back as you face the sail. This is the **back-to-wind position**. It is the easiest way to uphaul the rig. (You will use the back-to-wind position to start and complete most on-the-water maneuvers.)

In the uphaul stance, your feet should be in a comfortable stance straddling the mast no more than shoulder width apart. **Don't move your feet during the uphauling sequence**.

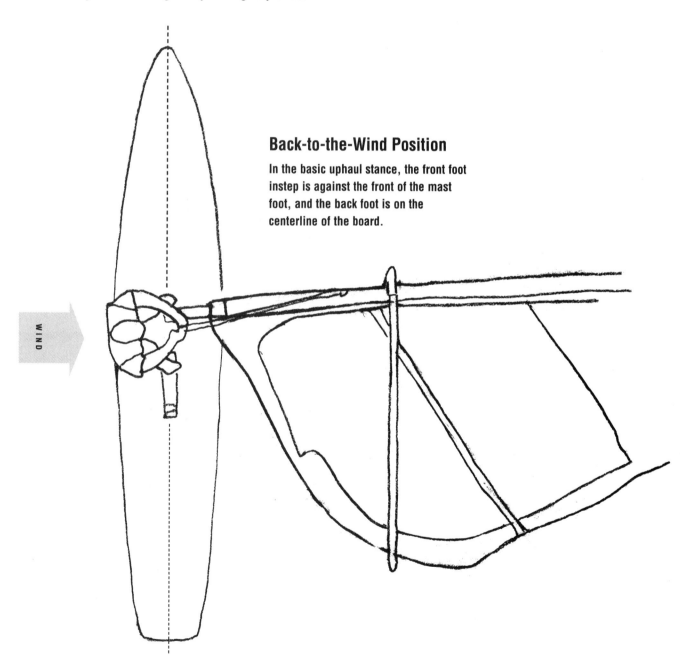

Back-to-the-Wind Position

In the basic uphaul stance, the front foot instep is against the front of the mast foot, and the back foot is on the centerline of the board.

WIND

Uphauling Sequence with Rig DOWNWIND

1 Put front foot instep against front of mast foot and back foot shoulder-width away on centerline; grab uphaul and bend your knees. Adjust your hands on the uphaul so your arms and back are straight.

2 Keeping arms and back straight, push up with thigh muscles and lean out just a bit. When top of mast is level with head, begin moving hand-over-hand up the uphaul line. Place both hands on the mast below the boom.

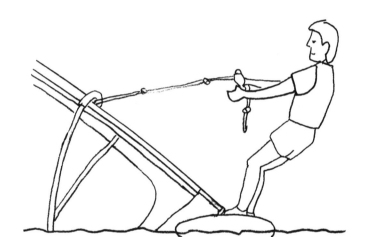

3 Front of boom is now level with your head; sail is flagging downwind; board is sideways to the wind; your back is to the wind. You are in the **basic position**, ready to start sailing.

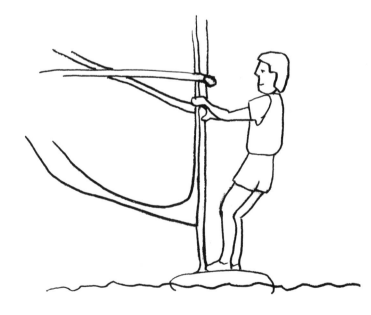

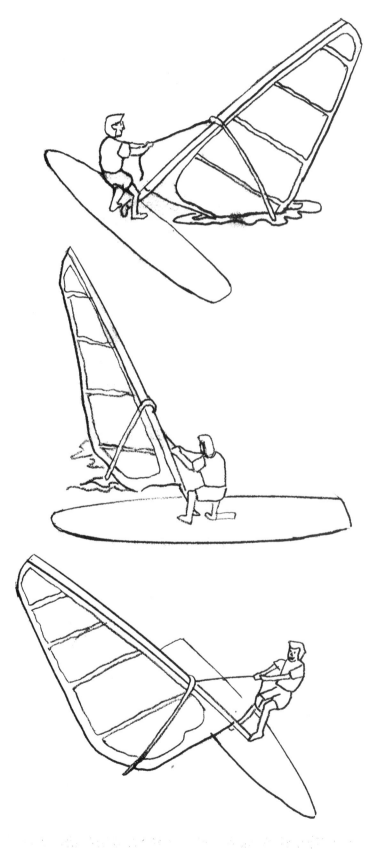

Uphauling Sequence with Rig UPWIND

Sometimes, the rig may end up lying **upwind** of the board. The top of the mast will point toward the wind and you will feel the wind blowing on your front as you face the sail.

1 Start uphauling as you would if the rig were lying downwind (Steps 1 and 2 opposite, page 54) until the top of the mast is level with or a little higher than your head. You will feel the rig being pushed toward the front or back of the board. Stop there! (Your hands should be at least half-way up uphaul.) Do not move your feet.

2 Keep mast fixed in front of you with back end of the sail and boom still in the water. Do not move feet. Wind will blow on sail and spin board around until the sail is flagging downwind.

3 Straighten body and move hand-over-hand to top of uphaul. Place hands on mast below the boom. You are once again in the **basic position**.

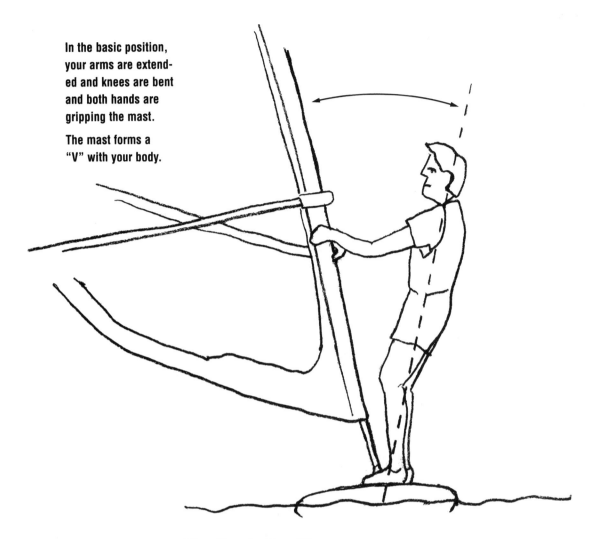

In the basic position, your arms are extended and knees are bent and both hands are gripping the mast.

The mast forms a "V" with your body.

The Basic Position

In the **basic position** your front foot instep is against the mast foot and your back foot is on the centerline of the board, a shoulder-width back from your front foot. Arms are extended and knees bent. Both hands hold onto the mast about six-to-eight inches below the boom.

All basic windsurfing maneuvers begin from the basic position, but you can also use it to take short rests while you relax or review your progress. For that reason, it is important that you know how to maintain this position—to keep the board sideways to the wind.

If the board begins to turn, it's because you have allowed the sail to move too far toward the front or back of the board. Just straighten your arms in front of you, being sure to keep the sail out of the water, and the board will swing back to the basic position (sideways to the wind) with the sail flagging downwind.

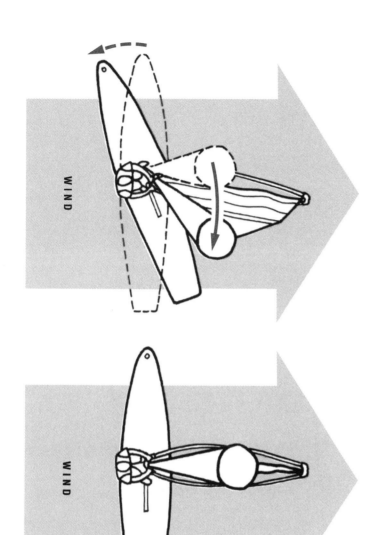

Maintaining the Basic Position

To turn the front of the board toward the wind, move the sail toward the back of the board.

To bring the board back to the basic position, move the sail straight out in front of you.

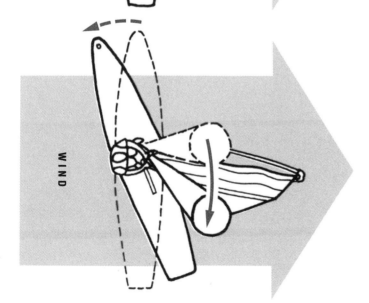

To turn the front of the board away from the wind, move the sail toward the front of the board. To bring the board back to the basic position, move the sail straight out in front of you again.

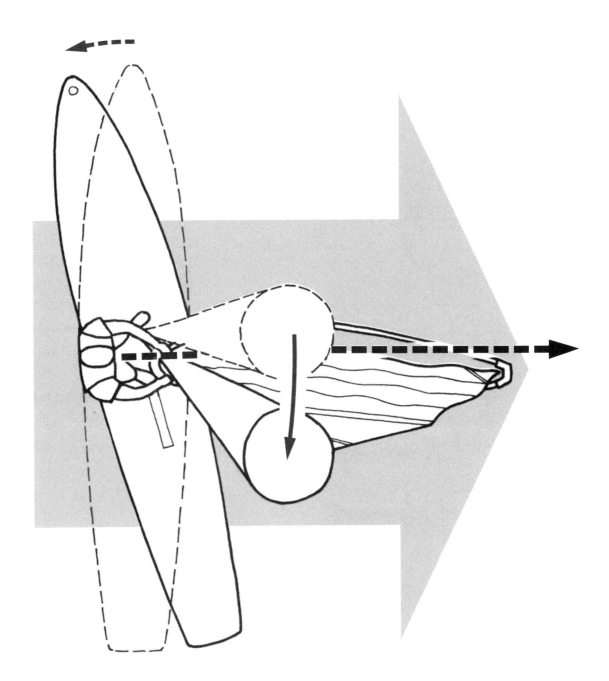

Turning the Board in the Basic Position

While in the basic position, the board can be turned to point the front (bow) in the opposite direction from where you started (a 180-degree turn). This is useful if you have uphauled your rig, only to find yourself pointed in the direction opposite where you want to go. Use the following sequence to turn your board. Repeating this maneuver a few times is also a great way to get your "sea legs."

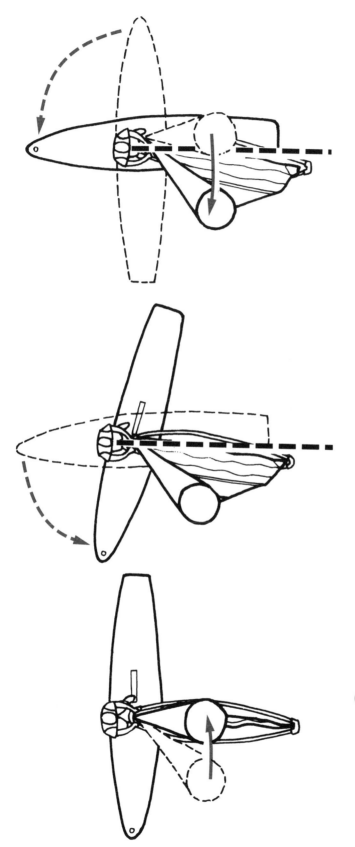

Sequence for 180-degree Turn while in the Basic Position:

1 From basic position (see diagram on opposite page); look at a landmark that is directly downwind (in line with the flagging sail) at eye level. Keeping arms straight, move rig toward back of board. The front (bow) of the board will begin turning toward the wind. Keep your vision locked on the downwind landmark. This will ensure your back is always toward the wind.

2 When you feel the board start to move let it rotate by alternately lifting front and back feet keeping your toes pointing toward the back end (clew) of the sail. Continue leaning rig in same direction until board has rotated 180 degrees. As board rotates, keep arms straight and keep looking at the downwind landmark to maintain back-to-wind position.

3 Stop board from rotating by centering mast or moving it momentarily toward back (stern). Move front foot against mast foot and return to stance and grip of basic position.

Getting Underway

It takes a sequence of five movements to go from the basic position to the **sailing position**. At first, each movement will be performed as a separate and deliberate component of a sequence. But in a very short time, the sequence will blend together into one fluid movement.

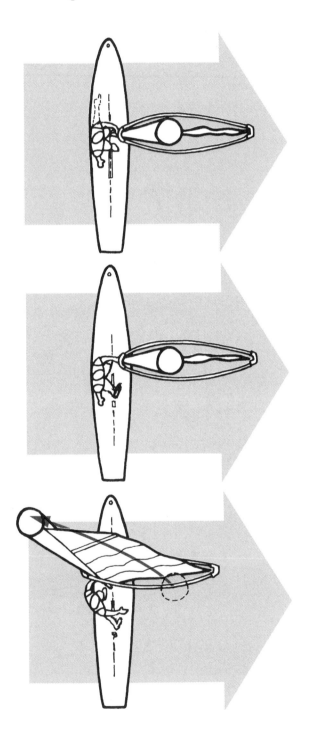

Movement 1:

From basic position, check sailing area for obstacles, then select a point dead ahead to sail toward. Point at it with front hand. Release back hand from mast and lower it to your side.

Movement 2:

Take a step back along centerline with your heel on the centerline and your toe slightly forward. Turn front foot so that it points to front (bow) and bring it back close to and behind the mast. Sail is still flagging without power.

Movement 3:

Pull rig across the board between your body and the front (bow) until rig feels light and balanced. Mast has passed through upright position to windward. Your weight is on your back foot. The sail is still flagging without power. This is balance position.

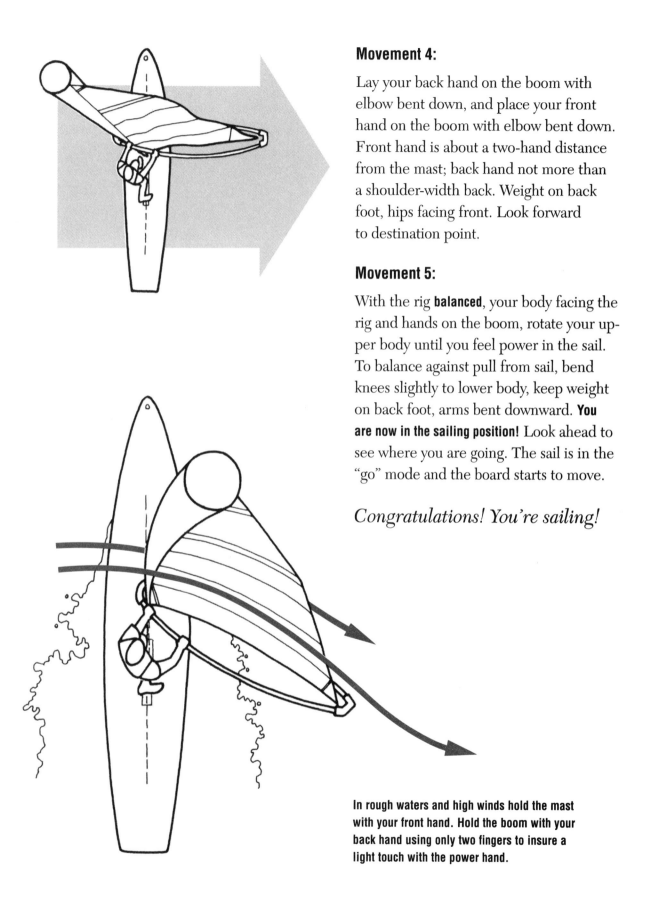

Movement 4:

Lay your back hand on the boom with elbow bent down, and place your front hand on the boom with elbow bent down. Front hand is about a two-hand distance from the mast; back hand not more than a shoulder-width back. Weight on back foot, hips facing front. Look forward to destination point.

Movement 5:

With the rig **balanced**, your body facing the rig and hands on the boom, rotate your upper body until you feel power in the sail. To balance against pull from sail, bend knees slightly to lower body, keep weight on back foot, arms bent downward. **You are now in the sailing position!** Look ahead to see where you are going. The sail is in the "go" mode and the board starts to move.

Congratulations! You're sailing!

In rough waters and high winds hold the mast with your front hand. Hold the boom with your back hand using only two fingers to insure a light touch with the power hand.

Basic Sailing Position

Look ahead over the front (bow) of the board

Hands not more than shoulder-width apart

Arms bent with elbows down; hold boom parallel to shoulders; equal pull on both hands

Straight back balanced against sideways pull of sail to form a "V" with the mast

Hips and bottom tucked in

Back leg slightly bent to act as a shock absorber

Back heel on centerline with toe slightly forward, shoulder-width from front foot

Weight on back foot

Front leg almost straight

Front foot pointed at bow, positioned behind the mast foot

Controlling Your Sail

Think of the sail as a swinging door with your back hand on the door handle or knob and your front hand holding the door near the hinges. By rotating your shoulders and hips in one unit, you can "open" and "close" the "door." This motion controls your speed, helps to set the sail to the correct wind angle, and enables you to release some pressure when the sail's power is too great.

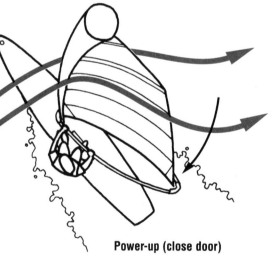

If you want to slow down, open the "door" to let the power escape (**depower**). The front edge of the sail will lose its shape and become flat. If the sail has few or no battens, the sail will start flapping (**luffing**). To speed back up again, rotate your shoulders and hips closing the door and powering up the sail. If the "door" closes too far, the sail will stall causing the board to travel sideways and even backwards. To get the best power and performance from the sail, you should open and close the sail between its luffed and stalled positions.

If a puff comes and starts to overpower you, open the door a little to depower and stay in control. When the puff leaves, close the "door" to power-up again.

If a really big puff hits you, use the **fail-safe maneuver** to stay in control. Release your back hand completely from the boom. The "door" is now open all the way. The sail will flag downwind, creating no power at all, and you will be in control. To start sailing again, return to the sailing position.

Power-up (close door)

Depower (open door)

Trimming your Sail

When you first start sailing, your board will be pointing across (perpendicular to) the wind. The "door" (sail) will be closed about half-way. When you sail further away from the wind (downwind), the "door" (sail) will be open more than half-way. When you sail closer to the wind (upwind), the "door" (sail) will be closed more than half-way.

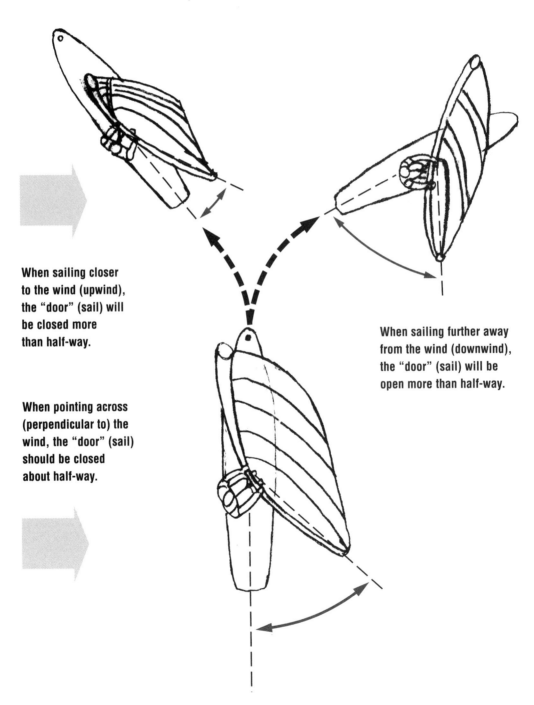

When sailing closer to the wind (upwind), the "door" (sail) will be closed more than half-way.

When pointing across (perpendicular to) the wind, the "door" (sail) should be closed about half-way.

When sailing further away from the wind (downwind), the "door" (sail) will be open more than half-way.

You must be careful that you don't close the sail too much. It's easy to make this mistake in the beginning. **Closing the sail too much** will inhibit the wind from flowing smoothly along both sides of the sail (called **stalling**). When this happens, you will notice a decrease in speed, a stronger pull on your front hand, and the sail will begin to lose its shape along the front edge. Try opening the sail a little. If your speed increases, this is a good indication that you had your sail closed too much. After each maneuver, re-check your sail position. Over-closing your sail is a common mistake.

Sail control is a measure of good balance and technique. Proper coordination of these elements is more important than muscle power. Sail control is a technique — not a physical exercise.

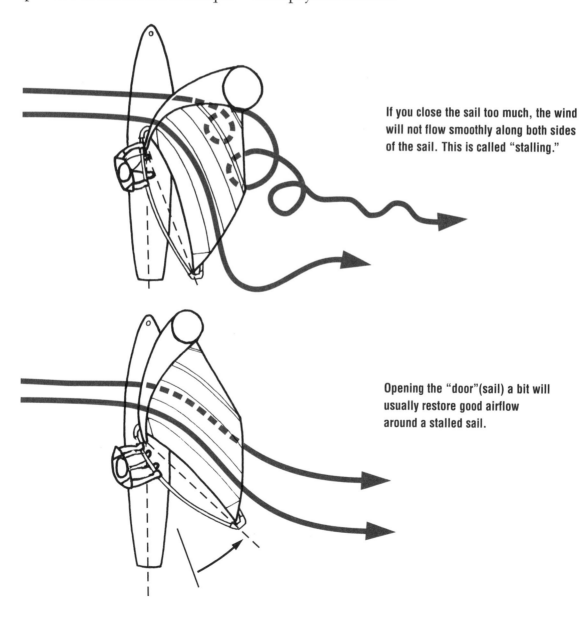

If you close the sail too much, the wind will not flow smoothly along both sides of the sail. This is called "stalling."

Opening the "door" (sail) a bit will usually restore good airflow around a stalled sail.

Steering

We have discussed how to control the power of the sail by moving it like a swinging door. The second way you use the sail is to steer the board by moving the sail either toward the front or back of the board when sailing.

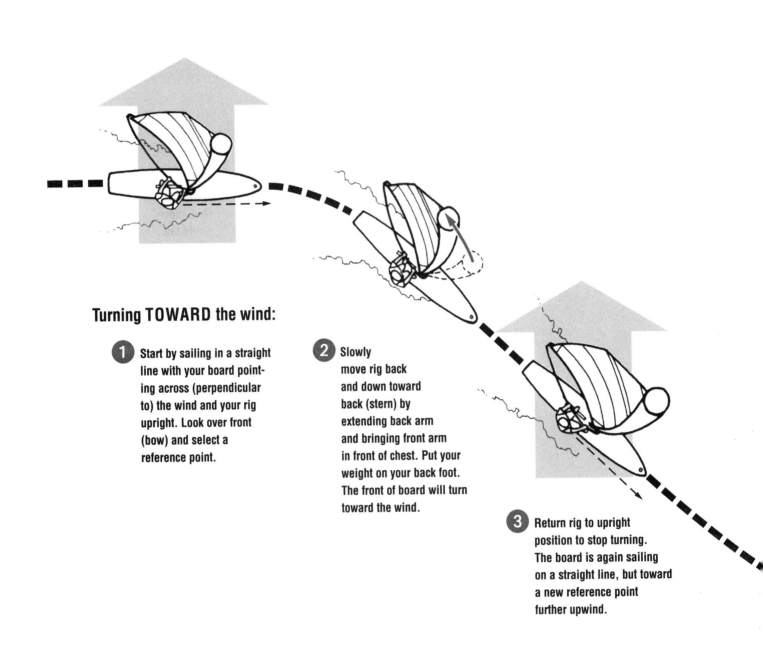

Turning TOWARD the wind:

1 Start by sailing in a straight line with your board pointing across (perpendicular to) the wind and your rig upright. Look over front (bow) and select a reference point.

2 Slowly move rig back and down toward back (stern) by extending back arm and bringing front arm in front of chest. Put your weight on your back foot. The front of board will turn toward the wind.

3 Return rig to upright position to stop turning. The board is again sailing on a straight line, but toward a new reference point further upwind.

If you move the sail toward the back (stern) of the board, the front of the board will turn toward the wind. If you move the sail toward the front (bow) of the board, the front of the board will turn away from the wind.

Whenever you are steering toward or away from the wind, always keep:

- Front foot behind and close to mast, pointed at bow
- Back foot across board on centerline and a shoulder-width from front foot
- Legs are relaxed, not stiff
- Hips and bottom tucked in
- Straight back balanced against sideways pull of sail
- Hands not more than shoulder-width apart
- Head held high and turned to look forward over bow

STEERING TIPS:

To turn toward the wind, move the sail toward the stern of the board.

To turn away from the wind, move the sail toward the bow of the board.

Turning AWAY the wind:

4 Move both hands about three inches back on boom, then firmly move rig to windward side of the board and slightly forward by extending front arm and moving back arm in front of chest. Without leaning forward, put your weight on front foot. Bend legs to lower your center of gravity; front of board will turn away from the wind.

5 Return rig to upright position; board sails on a straight line to a new reference point further downwind.

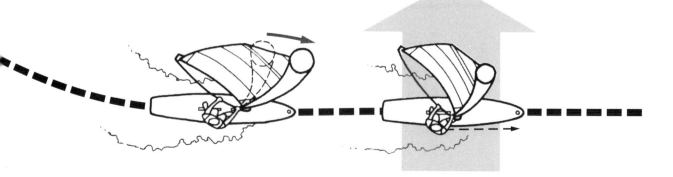

Stopping

To stop the board, you need to get rid of all the power in the sail-to depower it completely. This can be done by letting the sail flap (luff) like a flag, or by dropping the sail in the water.

The first level of stopping is the **controlled stop**. Start with the fail-safe maneuver—releasing your back hand from the boom and letting your front arm straighten downwind so the sail is flagging with no power in it. Lean your shoulders gently back into the wind as you bring your feet back to the basic position and your hands to the uphaul or the mast. The board will slow down to a drift.

To Stop

Simply release your back hand from the boom and let the sail flag downwind with no power.

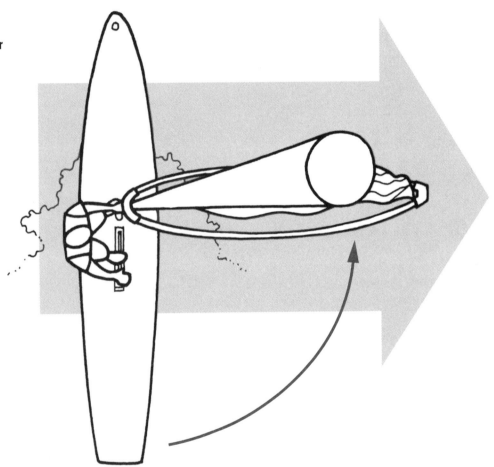

Controlled Drop

If you want to stop completely, simply drop the rig into to water. There is a tradeoff to this approach, however, because the mast can fall either toward the back or front of the board. If you want to uphaul the rig again, it is much easier when the mast is facing toward the front (bow) and the clew (back corner of sail) is toward the back (stern). This rig position is also much better for making rig adjustments or de-rigging for self-rescue.

To make sure that the rig ends up with the mast facing the front of the board, use the **controlled drop** method.

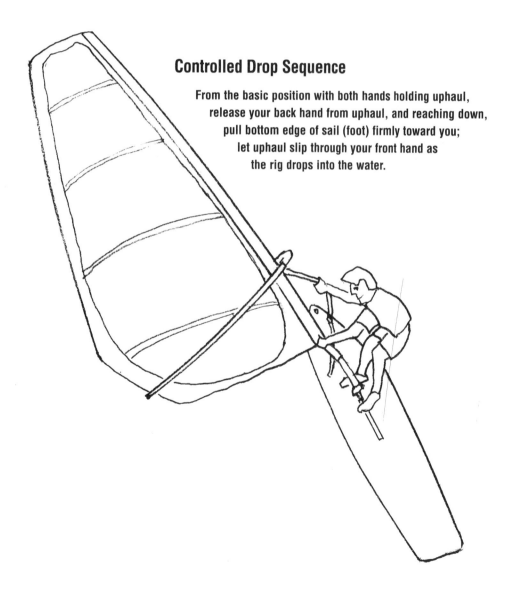

Controlled Drop Sequence

From the basic position with both hands holding uphaul, release your back hand from uphaul, and reaching down, pull bottom edge of sail (foot) firmly toward you; let uphaul slip through your front hand as the rig drops into the water.

Sailing Upwind

KEY CONCEPTS covered in this chapter:

- **No-go zone**
- **Centerboard, sail and body positions**
- **Steering**
- **Tacking**

One of your first priorities is to learn to sail toward the wind—**upwind** or **to windward**. When you are learning how to sail, you will often find yourself drifting or being blown downwind, or with the wind. It is imperative to know how to sail upwind so you can return to where you started.

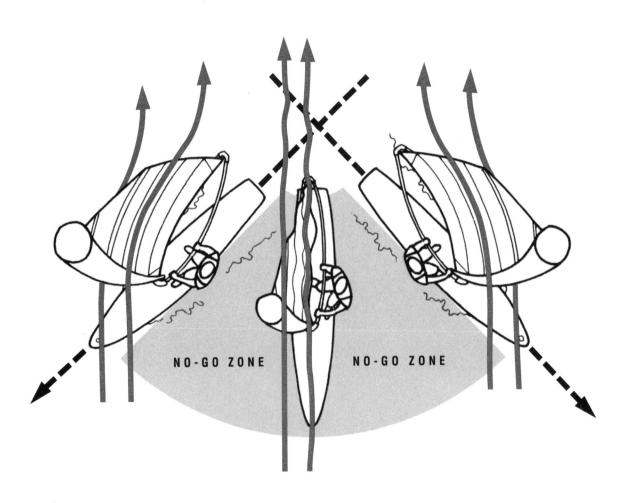

NO-GO ZONE   NO-GO ZONE

A board cannot sail directly into the wind. If you try it, the sail will luff and stall, and you would quickly come to a stop. This area is called the **no-go zone**. The closest a board can sail toward the wind is at an angle of about 45 degrees. This is your **upwind wind angle — 45 degrees**.

Sailing upwind, your centerboard should be in the down position and the sail closed, or pulled in, so that the back end of the boom is positioned close to the leeward side of the board. This upwind position is called **close-hauled**.

Use the same stance and grip for the sailing position, and watch for puffs, lulls and changes in wind direction. If you see a dark-looking patch on the water (puff) coming toward you, be ready to lean out and/or open the sail a little.

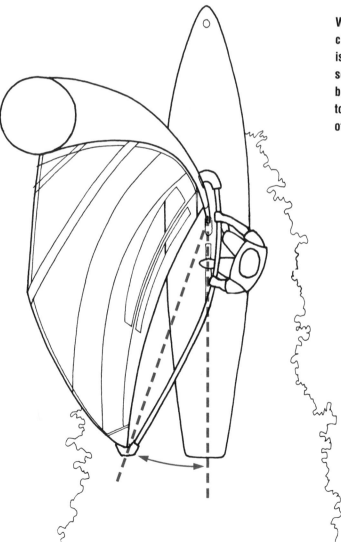

When sailing close-hauled, the sail is closed, or pulled in, so the back end of the boom is positioned close to the leeward side of the board.

Steering is important while sailing close-hauled. If you steer too close to the wind, into the no-go zone, the sail will start to stall or luff, and you will slow down and drift sideways. If you steer too far away from the wind, you may go faster but won't make good progress toward your upwind (windward) destination.

To find the **upwind "groove"**—the track that is the best combination of speed and upwind progress—start by gently moving the rig toward the back of the board. The board will turn slowly (**head up**) toward the wind. If you look at the forward edge of the sail where it curves just behind the mast, you will see that it is losing its shape and is being pushed toward you. This means that your sail is starting to stall and lose its power. You are beginning to enter the no-go zone. If you gently move the rig forward a little, the board will turn out of the no-go zone and the sail will regain its shape and power. You will regain speed and maneuverability.

Steering your board on the **perfect track "in the groove"**—will take some practice. The best advice is to make only small adjustments as you steer. Turn the board toward the wind until the sail just starts to stall, then turn away from the wind to the point where the sail stops stalling. Then look for a landmark to steer for that is in line with the front (bow). Since wind direction and strength rarely stay the same, you should repeat this maneuver fairly often to make sure that you are sailing at the optimum upwind angle.

Board "in the groove"—steer for landmark.

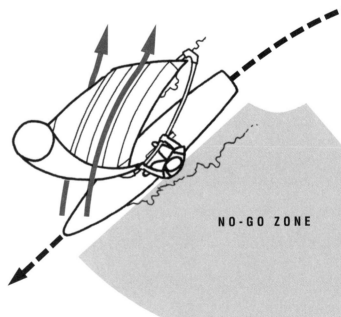

NO-GO ZONE

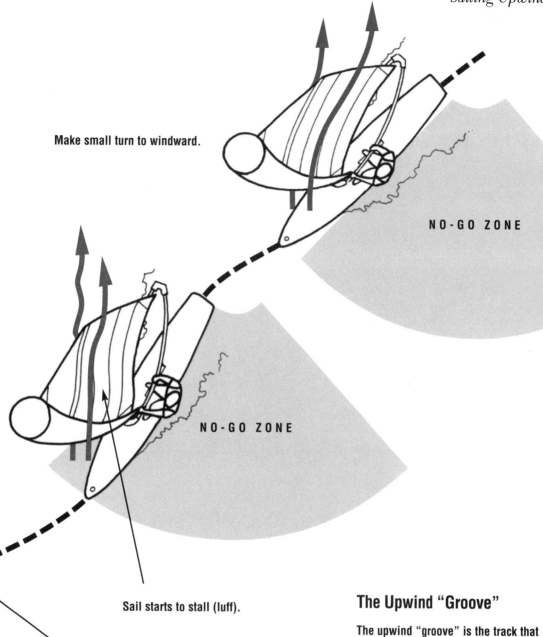

Make small turn to windward.

NO-GO ZONE

NO-GO ZONE

Sail starts to stall (luff).

Make small turn away from wind until sail just stops stalling.

The Upwind "Groove"

The upwind "groove" is the track that combines speed with good progress toward the wind.

To stay in the upwind groove, you periodically turn toward the wind until the sail just begins to stall and lose power—then turn back away from the wind just enough for your sail to stop stalling.

You will notice experienced sailors steering this subtle "S" course when sailing upwind.

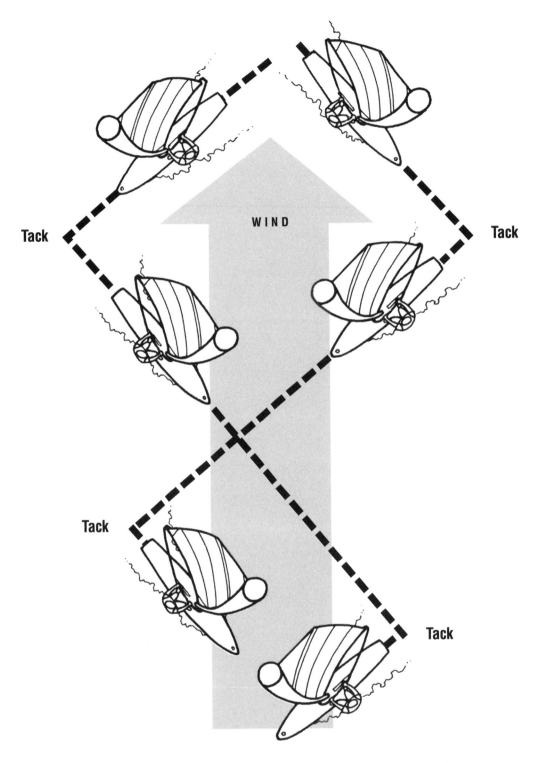

You can not sail directly into the no-go zone, but by sailing a "zigzag" course at 45 degrees to the wind, with the wind first on one side of the board then on the other, you can make progress toward the wind or toward your windward destination point.

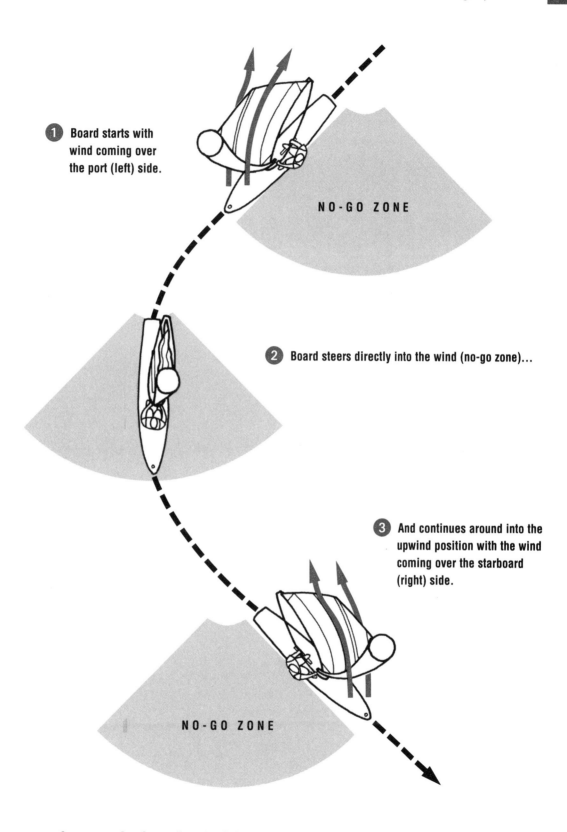

1 Board starts with wind coming over the port (left) side.

NO-GO ZONE

2 Board steers directly into the wind (no-go zone)...

3 And continues around into the upwind position with the wind coming over the starboard (right) side.

NO-GO ZONE

The maneuver of turning the front (bow) of the board through the wind, or no-go zone, as you switch from sailing with the wind on one side to the other is called **tacking**.

TACKING TIPS:

- Keep looking forward.

- Move smoothly, not abruptly.

- Shift back foot only AFTER the bottom of the sail makes contact with your back leg.

- Move your back foot first.

- Change hands on the mast and extend the mast arm quickly as you cross around the front of the mast.

- As you resume sailing position, quickly check your windward reference point.

In *Chapter 7 – Your First Sail*, you learned how to turn the bow through the wind, or no-go zone, from the basic position — a slow process. Now, you're going to learn to tack from the sailing position. By using the forward speed of the board, you will be able to turn through the no-go zone without stopping.

Tacking combines two previously learned skills, turning the board toward the wind and going to the sailing position, with a new one: stepping around the front of the mast.

Going to Sailing Position

6 Move back foot into the across-the-centerline position and turn front foot so foot, hips and body are facing bow (sailing position stance). Sail is flapping downwind.

7 Look forward and pull rig across board with mast (front) hand. Back hand grabs boom, front hand grabs boom; then pull in back hand to close the sail. You have returned to the sailing position.

Turning toward Wind

1 From sailing position, look over bow; grab mast with front hand (8-to-10 inches below boom) and let backhand slide about 4 inches forward on the boom.

2 With front arm straight, and weight on back foot, move rig back and down until boom end is about three feet off water. Board starts to turn toward wind. Keep looking over bow.

Stepping around Mast

3 Hold this turning stance as the board continues to turn until bottom of sail presses hard on back leg, then bring back foot forward a small step.

4 Swing front foot around front of mast as far as you can; you are still looking over the bow. Release back hand from boom and change hands on mast.

5 Extend mast (front) arm directly in front of you and quickly bring back foot as close to and as far around the mast as you can. The board continues to turn. You are now on opposite side of board and front (bow) is pointed in opposite direction on new tack.

WIND

9 Sailing Downwind

KEY CONCEPTS covered in this chapter:

- **Using a reference point**
- **Centerboard, sail and body positions**
- **Steering**
- **Jibing**
- **Running techniques**

Your first hours on the water were spent learning the basic board handling skills by sailing on a **beam reach** (board sideways to the wind) and then sailing upwind. But you also need to learn how to sail downwind — with the wind coming from behind the board — so you can sail to destinations that are to leeward of you.

If you are on a beam reach and you turn the board away (or bear off) with the wind, you will go from a beam reach to a **broad reach** and then to a downwind position where the front (bow) is pointing directly

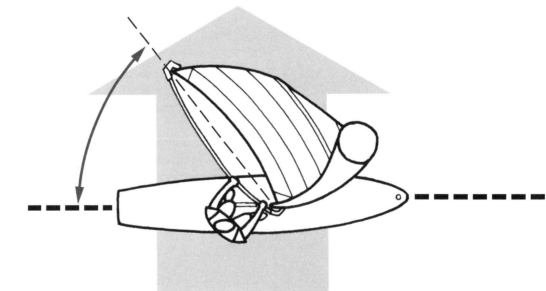

BEAM REACH

Wind coming over side of board. Sail is half-way open.

downwind and the wind is coming from behind the back (stern) of the board. Called a **run**, or running with the wind, it is a slow way to sail and you won't use it too often.

Using a reference point when steering or to orient yourself to the wind direction is just as important when sailing downwind as it is sailing upwind.

On a **beam reach** or **broad reach**, the normal sailing position is used and the sail is positioned about halfway out on a beam reach and three-quarters of the way out on a broad reach. The centerboard is kept in the down position at this basic level in light wind.

In your first lesson you learned how to steer by moving the rig back and down toward the stern to turn the board toward the wind, and moving the rig toward the bow to turn the board away from the wind. This technique is also used when sailing on a beam reach and broad reach.

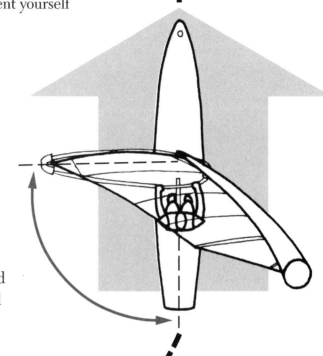

RUN

Wind coming over stern (back) of board. Sail is all the way open.

BROAD REACH

Wind coming over rear quarter of board. Sail is three-quarters open.

Jibing

If you change direction so that your front (bow) passes through the directly downwind position, the wind direction will swing around behind you from one side to the other. As this happens, you have to swing the sail from one side to the other (just as you do when you go from one tack to another while sailing upwind). Swinging the sail from one side to the other while sailing downwind is called **jibing**. Jibing differs from tacking, though, because during a jibe, the sail crosses the bow while you stay behind the mast.

Jibing can be broken down into three parts:

1. Turning the board away from the wind
2. Flipping the sail across the bow
3. Going to the sailing position

While jibing:

- Keep looking over bow
- Move firmly and smoothly, not abruptly
    - Keep weight on front (windward) foot
    - Wait until front of board appears under bottom of sail before flipping sail
    - Before each jibe, be sure to check for boats and obstacles that may be downwind of you or hidden behind your sail.

Jibing occurs when the wind direction swings around behind you from one side to the other.

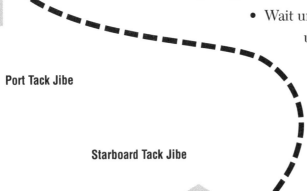

Port Tack Jibe

Starboard Tack Jibe

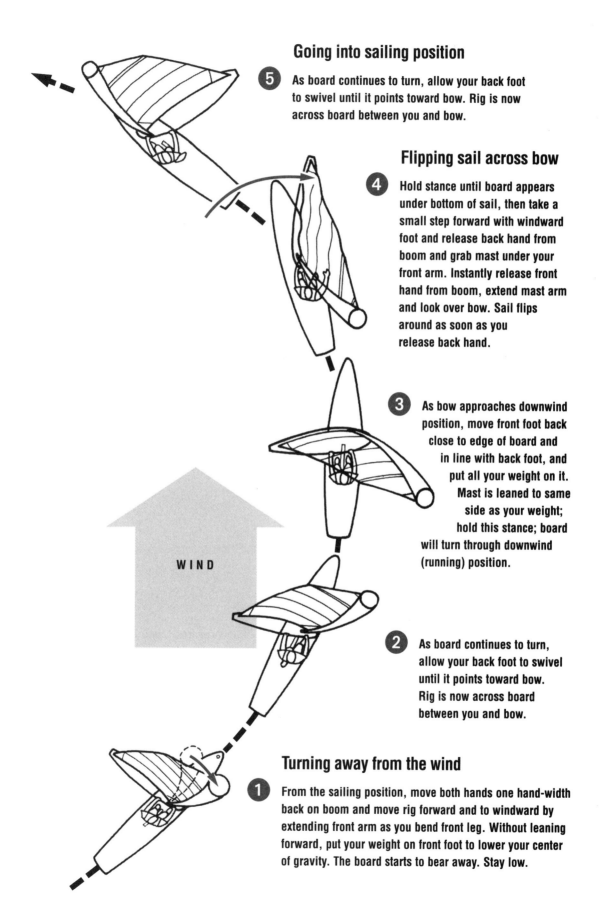

Going into sailing position

5 As board continues to turn, allow your back foot to swivel until it points toward bow. Rig is now across board between you and bow.

Flipping sail across bow

4 Hold stance until board appears under bottom of sail, then take a small step forward with windward foot and release back hand from boom and grab mast under your front arm. Instantly release front hand from boom, extend mast arm and look over bow. Sail flips around as soon as you release back hand.

3 As bow approaches downwind position, move front foot back close to edge of board and in line with back foot, and put all your weight on it. Mast is leaned to same side as your weight; hold this stance; board will turn through downwind (running) position.

WIND

2 As board continues to turn, allow your back foot to swivel until it points toward bow. Rig is now across board between you and bow.

Turning away from the wind

1 From the sailing position, move both hands one hand-width back on boom and move rig forward and to windward by extending front arm as you bend front leg. Without leaning forward, put your weight on front foot to lower your center of gravity. The board starts to bear away. Stay low.

Getting onto a Run

Turn onto a run by using the method for turning board away from wind. As bow approaches downwind position, bring front foot back close to side of board and half a step behind back foot; then quickly move back foot to opposite side of board; move rig back toward you and across board between your body and bow with mast leaning over one side and end of boom pointing out over other side; arms and legs are slightly bent.

3 Quickly move back foot opposite other foot and bring rig back and across board.

2 Bring front foot half a step behind back foot.

1 Turn away from wind.

Running Techniques

When sailing on a run, the board is pushed along by the wind. You will feel very little wind, if any at all, because you will be moving at a speed that is almost equal to the true wind. The sail will be positioned across the board perpendicular to the true wind so the wind can push against it. Because there is no sideways pull on the sail, a special position, the **running position**, is used. (*See diagram on next page.*)

"Survival" Sailing on a Run

If you can't handle the board and rig in rough water and winds, or if you are too tired, you can quickly sail downwind by using the Survival Run. Remember, the key is to keep the heels touching together on top of the centerline.

- Heels touch, on the centerline
- Toes outward slightly
- Legs well bent
- Back Straight
- Hips Forward
- Arms Straight
- Head high, look to the horizon
- Push the clew over the bow and keep it there.

Running Stance and Grip

- One foot on each side of the board, heels touching centerline.

- Legs bent.

- Rig is raked backwards between your body and bow with mast leaning over one side and end of boom pointing out over the opposite side.

- Hands not more than shoulder-width apart.

- Arms slightly bent with equal pull on boom.

- Head held high and looking forward through window of sail.

Balance

When you first try running downwind, the board may feel unstable and "tippy." But you will soon learn that once again the key to balance is to keep your legs loose and flexible as you use your body weight to balance the board.

The centerboard is kept in the down position. As you become more experienced, you will learn how to adjust the centerboard to minimize drag and increase performance. In rough water, retract centerboard slightly for better control.

A different steering technique is used on a run. Simply lean the rig to one side as you move your weight to the same side, the board will turn to the opposite side. To turn back again, lean the rig and shift your weight to the opposite side. *(See diagram on opposite page.)*

HOT TIP!

The key to balance is to keep your legs loose and flexible as you use your body weight to balance the board.

10 *Points of Sail*

KEY CONCEPTS covered in this chapter:

• **Points of sail**

Now that you have learned to maneuver upwind and downwind, the different points of sail should be reviewed. There are six general points of sail: the **no-go zone, close-hauled, close reach, beam reach, broad reach**, and **run**. Each point of sail covers a range of angles that the board sails in

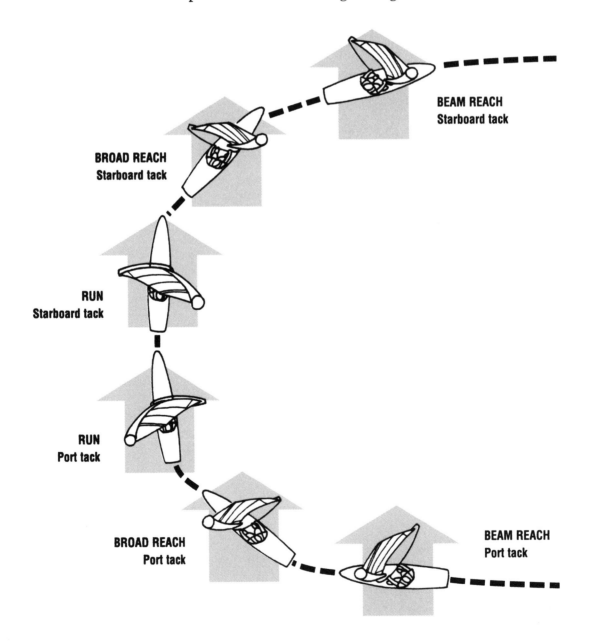

BEAM REACH
Starboard tack

BROAD REACH
Starboard tack

RUN
Starboard tack

RUN
Port tack

BROAD REACH
Port tack

BEAM REACH
Port tack

relation to the wind. For instance, you would be on a close reach, if you were sailing at a 55-, 60-, or 75-degree angle to the wind. Although some people have assigned arbitrary angles to depict the boundary line between adjoining points of sail—in reality, the transition line is approximate. What's important is for you to understand that if you sailed in a circle, you would pass through all of these points of sail.

Notice in the points of sail illustration that although the angle between the board and the wind changes, the sail always remains at the same angle to the wind, except on the run.

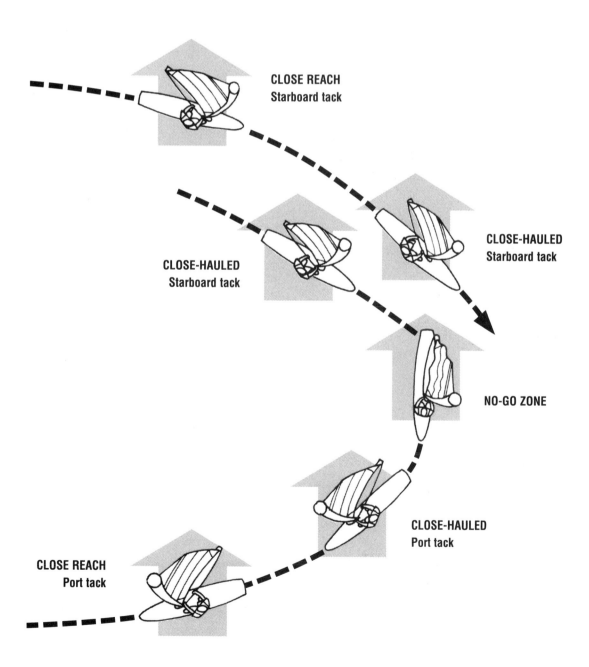

CLOSE REACH
Starboard tack

CLOSE-HAULED
Starboard tack

CLOSE-HAULED
Starboard tack

NO-GO ZONE

CLOSE-HAULED
Port tack

CLOSE REACH
Port tack

No-Go Zone

As your instructor has shown you, no sailing craft can sail directly into the wind. There is a **no-go zone** that extends approximately 45 degrees to either side of the wind. You can turn (tack) through this zone, but you can not sail in it. Your sail will flap (luff) and the board will slow down to a stop, and then start to drift with the wind. If you want to sail to a destination that is located in the no-go zone, you will have to sail diagonally (about 45 degrees) across the wind, tacking from one side of the no-go zone to the other to follow a zigzag route.

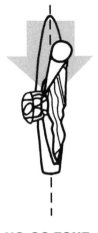

NO-GO ZONE

Sail flapping (luffing) and developing no power. Board stops.

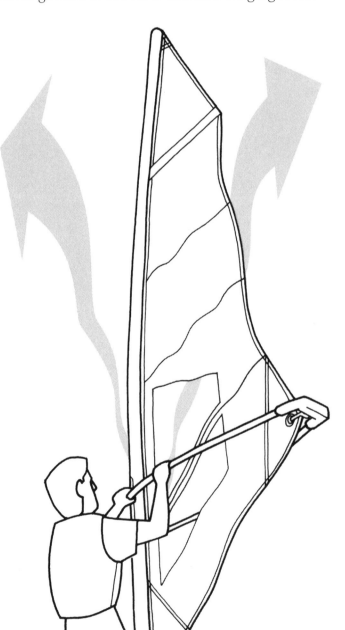

Close-hauled

When your sail (door) is pulled in (closed) and your board is sailing at approximately 45 degrees to the wind, you are sailing **close-hauled**. You are just on the outside edge of the no-go zone. This is the closest angle to the wind that you can sail a board without your sail stalling or luffing. Your sail will be in the **pull mode**, which means that all the power developed from the sail is generated from lift.

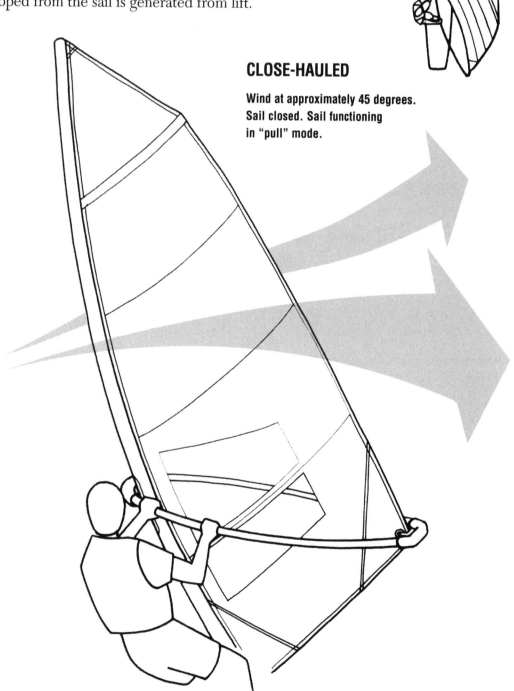

CLOSE-HAULED

Wind at approximately 45 degrees. Sail closed. Sail functioning in "pull" mode.

Close Reach

If you turn away from the wind a little, so that your board is no longer sailing **close-hauled**, you will sail onto a close reach. You are still making progress to windward, but it will take longer to work your way upwind.

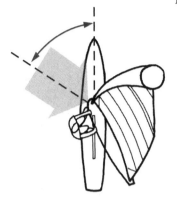

CLOSE REACH

Wind just forward of the side. Sail slightly open. Sail functioning in "pull" mode.

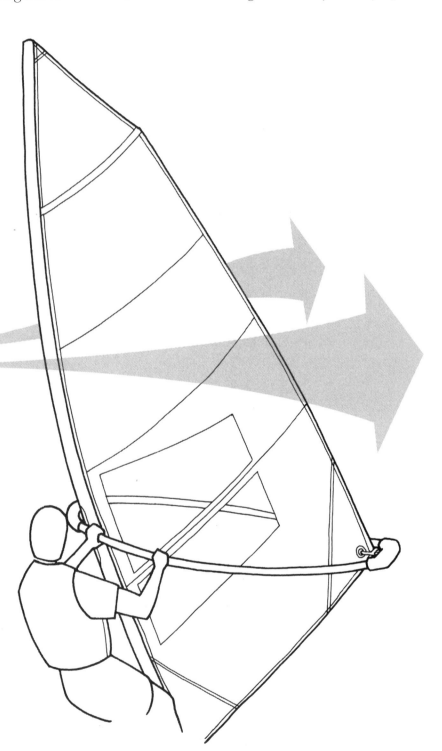

Beam Reach

If you continue to turn away from the wind until the board is across or sideways to the wind, you will be on a **beam reach**. You will not make any progress toward a windward destination, but it is a fast point of sail. In the right conditions, you can use it to get your board to rise up on top of the water and plane — a fast, fun, exhilarating thrill.

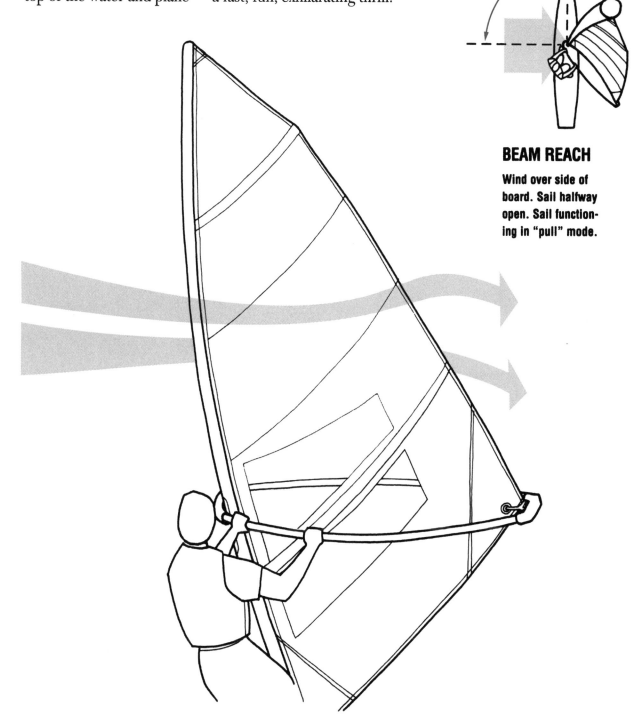

BEAM REACH

Wind over side of board. Sail halfway open. Sail functioning in "pull" mode.

Broad Reach

When you turn away from the wind while on a beam reach, you will sail onto a **broad reach**. This is the point of sail where most boards reach their maximum speed. Your sail will generate power from a combination of pull (lift) and push (wind-push). The wind will still flow past both sides of the sail producing lift, but more power also comes from the wind simply pushing on the windward side of the sail.

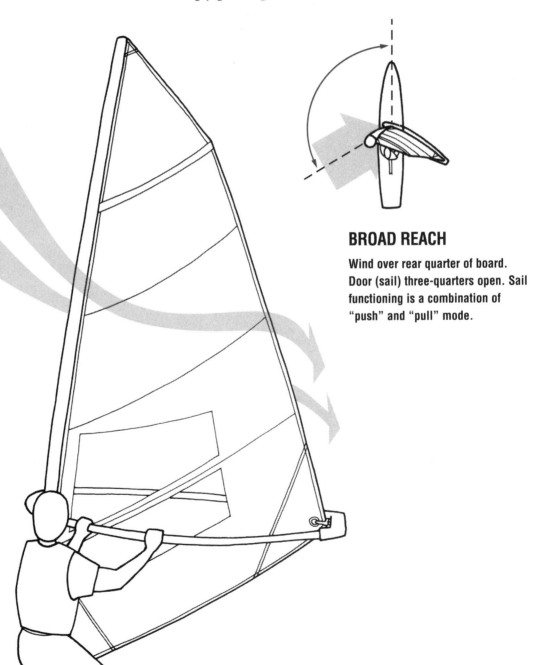

BROAD REACH

Wind over rear quarter of board. Door (sail) three-quarters open. Sail functioning is a combination of "push" and "pull" mode.

Run

When the wind is coming over the back (stern) of the board, you will be on a **run**. This is the slowest point of sail. Your sail is completely in the push mode with the wind pushing on one side of the sail—no lift (pull) is being created. It will feel as if the wind has stopped moving because your board will be moving in the same direction as the true wind, but as soon as you turn to sail upwind again, you will discover that the wind is still blowing as strong.

RUN

Wind coming over back (stern) of board. "Door" (sail) all the way open. Sail functioning totally in 'push' mode.

11 Launching & Landing

KEY CONCEPTS covered in this chapter:

- **Sailing off a beach**

- **Sailing off a dock**

The ideal wind direction for sailing off a beach is when the wind is blowing along (parallel to) the shore. You will be able to launch, sail out, turn around, and sail back to the beach — all with the wind coming from the side (beam reach). Launching and landing can be much more challenging when the wind is blowing onto the beach.

An important note: When launching or landing on a beach in waves, don't let the board get between you and the oncoming waves. You could get hurt if the board gets thrown against you, even by a small wave.

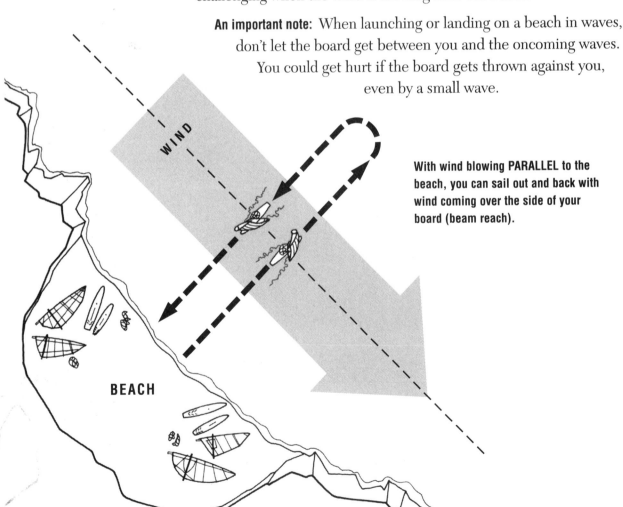

WIND

BEACH

With wind blowing **PARALLEL** to the beach, you can sail out and back with wind coming over the side of your board (beam reach).

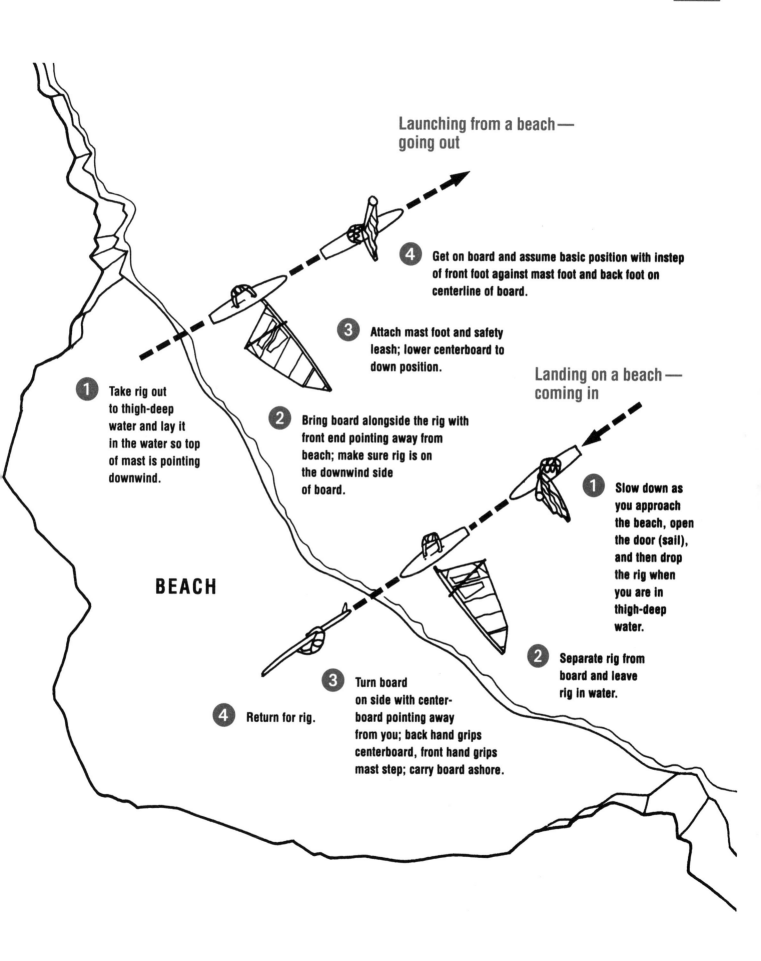

Launching from a beach— going out

1 Take rig out to thigh-deep water and lay it in the water so top of mast is pointing downwind.

2 Bring board alongside the rig with front end pointing away from beach; make sure rig is on the downwind side of board.

3 Attach mast foot and safety leash; lower centerboard to down position.

4 Get on board and assume basic position with instep of front foot against mast foot and back foot on centerline of board.

BEACH

Landing on a beach— coming in

1 Slow down as you approach the beach, open the door (sail), and then drop the rig when you are in thigh-deep water.

2 Separate rig from board and leave rig in water.

3 Turn board on side with centerboard pointing away from you; back hand grips centerboard, front hand grips mast step; carry board ashore.

4 Return for rig.

Sailing off a Dock

When sailing off a dock, use a low dock that is only 6-to-12 inches above the water. A dock any higher is difficult to launch from at the basic sailing level. If you have someone to help you, you can attach the rig to the board and lower the board into the water on the **leeward side of the dock**. If you are alone, use the alternative method described below.

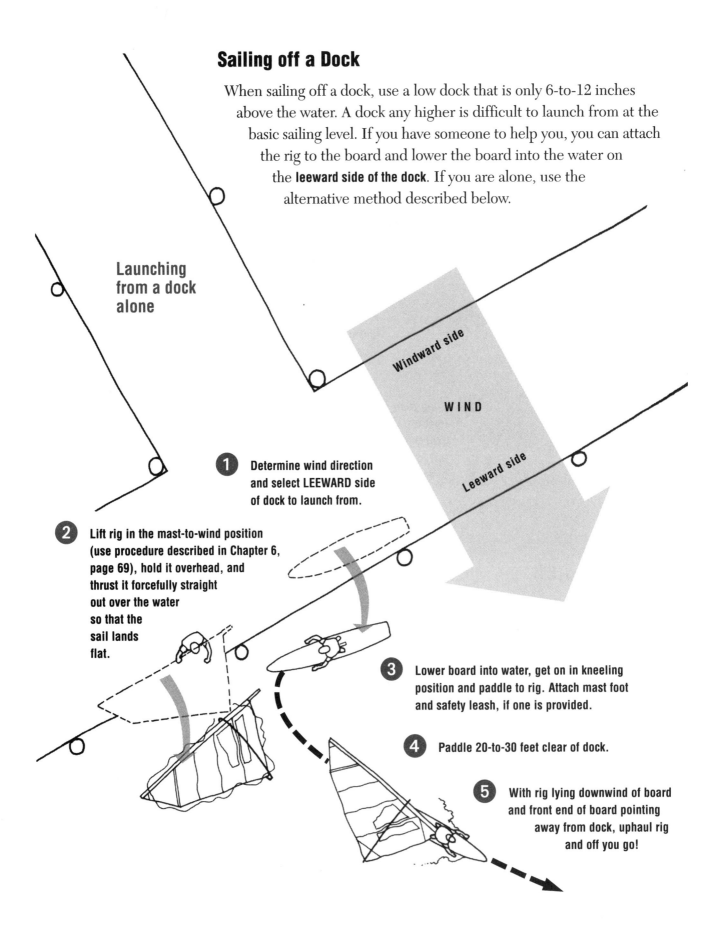

Launching from a dock alone

Windward side

W I N D

Leeward side

1 Determine wind direction and select LEEWARD side of dock to launch from.

2 Lift rig in the mast-to-wind position (use procedure described in Chapter 6, page 69), hold it overhead, and thrust it forcefully straight out over the water so that the sail lands flat.

3 Lower board into water, get on in kneeling position and paddle to rig. Attach mast foot and safety leash, if one is provided.

4 Paddle 20-to-30 feet clear of dock.

5 With rig lying downwind of board and front end of board pointing away from dock, uphaul rig and off you go!

Landing on a dock

3 Untie uphaul and lift rig, at boom attachment, onto dock keeping mast-to-wind.

2 Separate rig from board; tie rig to dock with uphaul; climb on dock; lift board onto dock using tow eye line (rope).

1 Drop rig in water about 20 feet from dock and paddle close to dock.

12 Rules of the Road

KEY CONCEPTS covered in this chapter:

- **Avoiding collisions**
- **Right-of-way**
- **Five basic rules**

There are maritime regulations that are designed to promote safety on the water and, most importantly, prevent collisions. Many of them apply to recreational watercraft. They are frequently referred to as **right-of-way rules** or "rules of the road."

Avoiding Collisions

There is always a possibility of running into someone or something. Remember to look around before you tack or jibe, and check for boats and obstacles to leeward that may be hidden behind your sail.

One of the best ways to avoid a collision is simply to change direction. You can also avoid a collision by slowing down or stopping your board. Whichever method you use, it is a good idea to do it early to let the other person know your intentions.

"Hey guys, I've got the right of way! GUYS!"

There may be times when it is easier for you — even though you have right-of-way — to change direction than for a large boat that is not as maneuverable. Even though it's an act of courtesy to change direction to stay clear of them, be sure to do it in plenty of time so you don't confuse the other boat and possibly cause a collision.

Right-of-Way

Whenever two boards (or a board and a boat) meet, one will have the right-of-way and the other will be required to stay clear. The right-of-way board is required to maintain its heading and speed so the other person can safely maneuver out of the way. Nevertheless, the person who has right-of-way should always be prepared to avoid a collision in case something prevents the other person from staying clear.

In encounters between sail craft, right-of-way is often determined by which tack you and the other person are on, **port** or **starboard**. When sailing on **port tack**, the wind is on the **left** (port) side of the board, and on **starboard tack** the wind is on the **right** (starboard) side. There is an easy way to determine this for a board. If you are on starboard tack, your right hand is closer to the mast; and on port tack, your left hand is closer to the mast.

Right is right!

When your RIGHT hand is closest to the mast you have RIGHT-of-way.

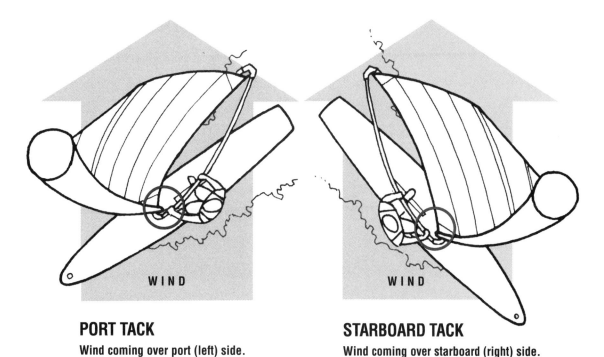

PORT TACK
Wind coming over port (left) side.
LEFT HAND is closer to mast.

STARBOARD TACK
Wind coming over starboard (right) side.
RIGHT HAND is closer to mast.

Basic Rule #1

When two boards, or a board and a sailboat, on different tacks meet (sails are on different sides), the board on starboard tack has right-of-way over the board on port tack. If you are on starboard tack, it is a good idea to hail the person on port tack by saying, "Starboard," or "I have right-of-way." This will remind them that you have right-of-way and they must stay clear.

Handy reminder!

A quick way to remember starboard (right) from port (left) is that the words PORT and LEFT both have four letters.

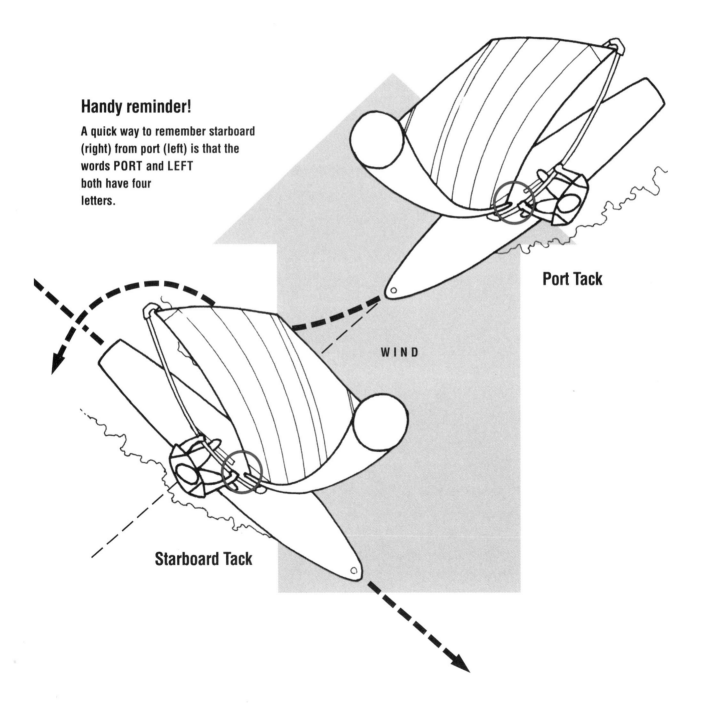

Port Tack

WIND

Starboard Tack

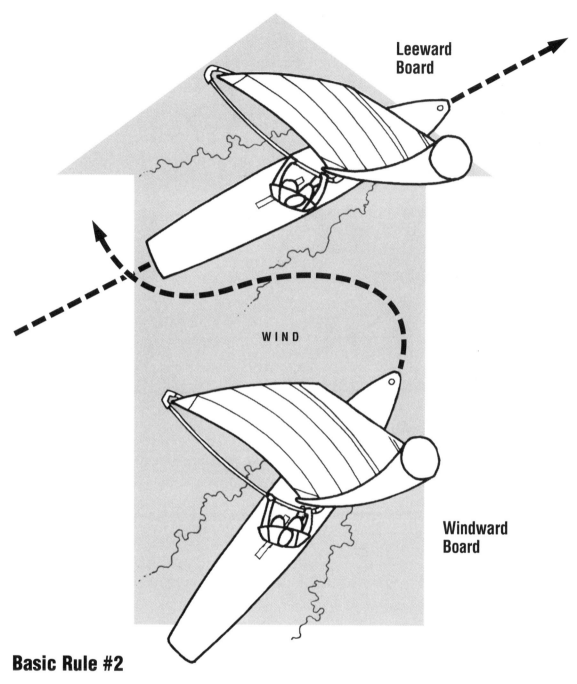

Leeward
Board

WIND

Windward
Board

Basic Rule #2

When two boards on the same tack converge, the leeward board has right-of-way over the windward board. For example, when two boards are both sailing on starboard tack but are on different points of sail (i.e., close reach and broad reach) that put them on a collision course, the board closer to the wind source must keep clear. The board further from the wind has right-of-way. If you are the leeward board, hail, "I'm leeward board—please stay clear," to remind the other person.

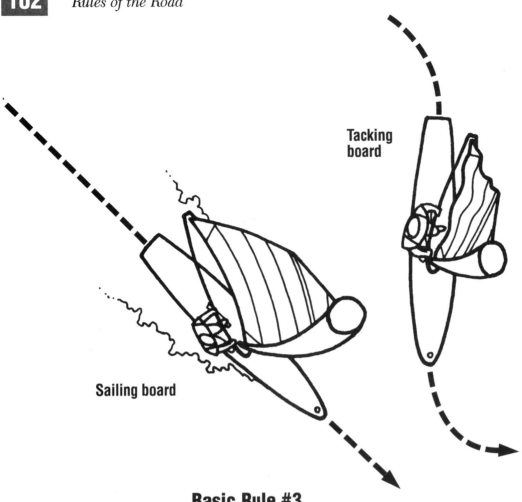

Tacking board

Sailing board

Basic Rule #3

A board sailing on port or starboard tack has right-of-way over any board that is tacking or jibing. If you are going to tack or jibe, make sure that the water around you is clear of other boats during your maneuver.

Basic Rule #4

When a board is overtaking another, the slower one has right-of-way. The slower board should hold its course to allow the overtaking board to pass around it.

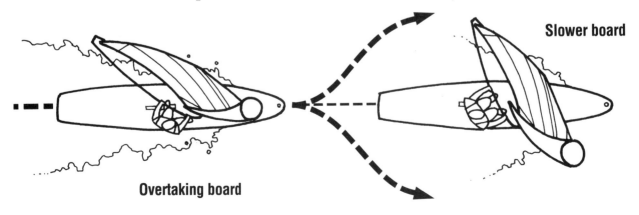

Slower board

Overtaking board

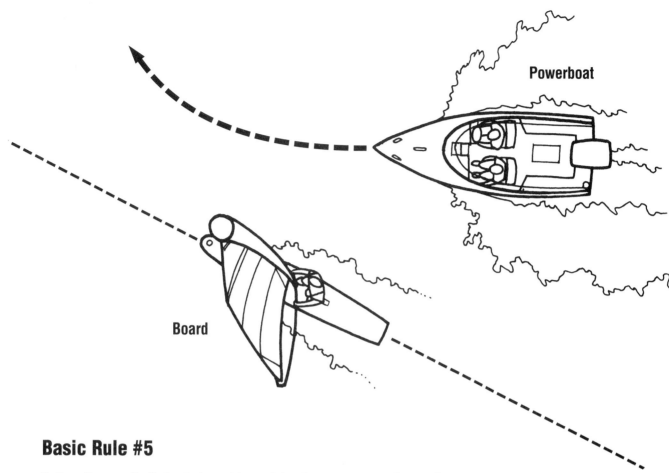

Basic Rule #5

Sail craft generally (but not always) have right-of-way over powerboats. One exception is when a board or sailboat meets a commercial vessel, such as a ship, ferry, tug, dredge, or fishing boat. These vessels are restricted in their ability to maneuver, because of their size or type of operation, and boards should stay well clear of them. Large recreational power-boats may also fall into this category if they have limited maneuverability due to their size and their need to operate in deep-water channels. Another exception is when a board is overtaking a powerboat (it happens!)—the board must stay clear.

Another category of boats that boards must stay clear of is manually powered boats, such as rowboats, canoes, and kayaks.

There is also an unspoken rule among sailors which should be considered part of your sailor's code. When two boards meet, it is common courtesy for the more experienced person to maneuver around the less experienced one.

And, finally—remember, **if in doubt, stay clear**.

13 Weather & Current

KEY CONCEPTS covered in this chapter:

- **High and low pressure systems**
- **Jet stream**
- **Wind movement**
- **Winds: cross-shore, onshore, and offshore**
- **Tides and currents**

Few sports are as weather dependent as windsurfing. As you gain sailing experience, you will discover that weather is constantly changing and that no two days are ever exactly the same. Even if the wind is blowing from the same direction as yesterday, the waves and wind speed will probably be different.

A smart, safe sailor quickly learns to identify the signs of good sailing weather and the warning signs of poor weather.

"Oh boy, wind!"

Getting Weather Information

You can obtain weather information from a variety of sources. In addition to the U.S. Coast Guard and the National Weather Service, newspapers, radio, television, and cable stations provide detailed weather maps, reports and forecasts. Some windsurfing shops also provide daily forecasts.

You will want to know wind speed and direction, existing and expected weather conditions, and tide and current information. Marine forecasts and aviation reports are the best sources for wind speed and warnings of poor weather. These are often available by telephone or you can buy a special marine weather radio. These are inexpensive and will give you 24-hour-a-day access to weather conditions and forecasts at the touch of a button.

One of the best devices for predicting weather is the barometer, which indicates pressure changes of different air masses. Generally, when the barometer is rising, it indicates fair weather and good sailing conditions. When the barometer starts to fall, poor weather may be on its way. Television weather reports usually give the barometric pressure and indicate whether it is rising or falling.

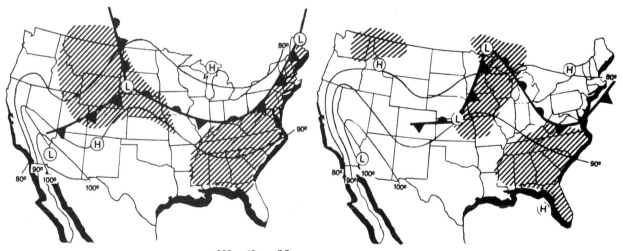

Weather Maps

Weather maps for two consecutive days show high-pressure (H) and low-pressure (L) systems moving across the country from west to east. Weather maps are found in many newspapers. The most up-to-date weather information is available from radio and television broadcasts.

Weather Systems

In North America, weather systems normally move from west to east. These systems are referred to as low and high pressure systems and may originate in Canada, the Pacific Ocean, the Gulf of Mexico, or even the Atlantic Ocean.

The **high-pressure system**, identified by a large "H" on the weather map, usually denotes drier, cooler air, and you can generally expect clear weather and good sailing conditions. The cool air tends to sink to the earth's surface and cause an increase in pressure and a rising reading on the barometer.

The **low-pressure system** is identified by an "L" on the weather map and usually denotes relatively warm air that has a tendency to rise, creating lower pressure and a fall in the barometer. Low-pressure systems can have strong winds, rain, and storms.

High-pressure systems

contain cool, dry air that sinks to the ground. When these systems meet warmer air masses, clouds, rain and strong winds can occur. The border where warm and cold masses meet is called a front.

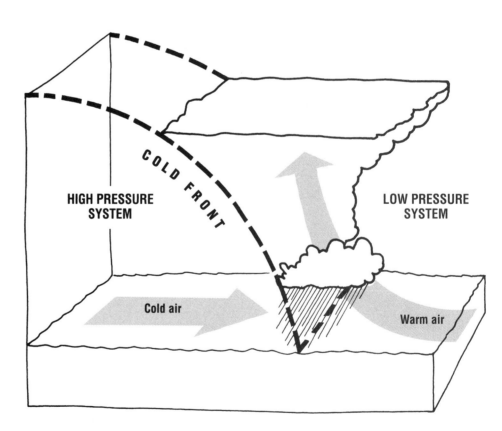

HIGH PRESSURE SYSTEM

COLD FRONT

LOW PRESSURE SYSTEM

Cold air

Warm air

High-pressure systems are generally associated with cumulus or high stratus type clouds, while the low-pressure system is generally associated with low level clouds. As a sailor, it is important to understand that clouds can move faster than the surface wind, which means the approaching weather system may first appear at higher altitudes. Fast-moving clouds may bring higher wind speeds, and slow-moving clouds lower winds.

The **jet stream** is a snake-like river of air that circles the earth about 35,000 feet above the surface. It controls the location and movement of the high- and low-pressure systems.

Wind Movement

Wind is created by pressure differences in the atmosphere, with air generally flowing from high pressure to low pressure areas. Wind also can be affected greatly by local topography. If you sail on a body of water surrounded by large buildings or hills, for instance, the wind speed and direction will change often. This is a unique aspect of

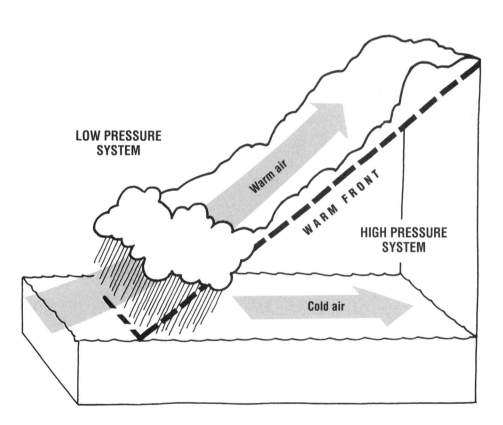

LOW PRESSURE SYSTEM

Warm air

WARM FRONT

HIGH PRESSURE SYSTEM

Cold air

Low-pressure systems contain relatively warm air that has a tendency to rise. They generally move more slowly than high-pressure systems and the rain and wind created when they meet cold air masses is less violent.

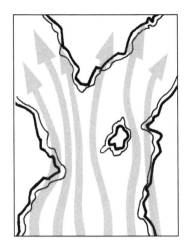

Wind can be affected greatly by local topography, large buildings and other obstacles.

sailing which is fun to discover and learn. Your environmental awareness will help you react to these changes.

Water and Wind

Generally, winds are referred to as cross-shore, onshore, and offshore. **Cross-shore winds** blow parallel to the shore, and are best for you because they will not carry you away from the beach. You simply sail out, turn around, and sail back to the shore-reaching both ways. This is the ideal wind direction for practicing your new found skills.

Onshore Winds

Onshore winds, or sea breezes, occur when hot air rising off the land draws cooler air in from the water. These breezes often are strongest in the afternoon on sunny days, when the land has had a chance to warm up the most.

WIND

Onshore winds, or sea breezes, occur when the air blows from the water onto the shore. On warm sunny days, these breezes can become quite strong in the afternoon, as the warm air rises over the land drawing in the cooler air from the sea. Waves hitting the shore are bigger in an onshore wind, and can make it difficult to launch and land on a beach. They can also toss your board around, causing damage or injury. Keep this in mind when getting your weather forecast.

Offshore winds blow from the land out onto the water and for this reason are most affected by local topography. Often when you stand on the beach, an offshore wind will seem relatively calm. But as you sail away from the beach, the wind will increase. When you try to return, you may discover that the wind is too strong for you to sail back against it. A smart sailor does not sail in offshore winds because of the high risk of getting into trouble and being blown out to sea—far away from land and rescue.

Onshore Wind
Blowing from water onto land. Will not blow you out to sea, but waves hitting shore can make launching and landing difficult.

Cross-shore Wind
Parallel to shore. Best for windsurfing. Will not carry you away from beach.

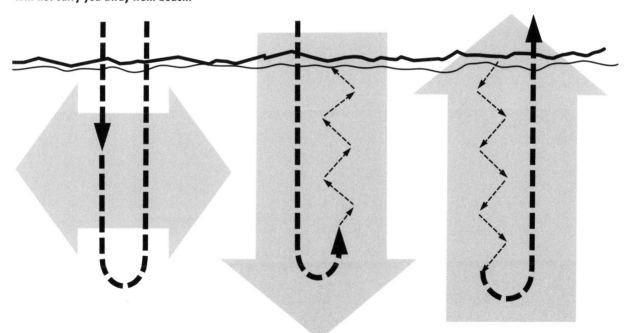

Offshore Wind
Blowing from land out onto water. Do NOT sail in offshore winds. If you get in trouble, you can be blown out to sea.

Windsurfing Breezes

When you are learning to sail, four-to-six knots of wind is ideal. This allows you to practice your maneuvers without being overpowered, and you will progress more quickly than if you tried to learn in more wind. As your skills improve with just a few hours of practice, you should be able to sail easily in winds up to 10 knots with confidence.

The relationship between wind speed and the pressure exerted on the sail is important for you to understand. If the wind increases from 5 knots to 10 knots, the pressure (power) on the sail is not just doubled, it multiplies by the square of the increase—in this case, a factor of four! This means that relatively small increases in wind are significant.

Cross-shore winds are what one hopes for. With the wind blowing parallel to the beach, you can launch easily and as soon as you get tired, it's easy to turn around and get back to shore. If the forecast indicates offshore breezes at your usual location, hop in the car and find a sailing spot that has cross-shore winds.

Where to Sail

In selecting a site for windsurfing, wind direction is important. In this diagram, locations B and D are ideal for windsurfing. A is not good—wind is offshore. C is not good—winds are onshore.

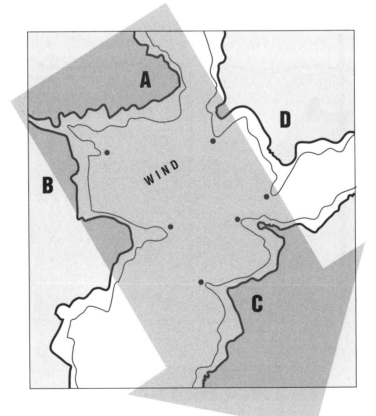

Signs in the Sky

A good sailor constantly monitors his or her surroundings, especially for any signs of threatening weather. Collecting weather information from television or radio is the first step to determining whether conditions are right for sailing. You should also know some of the early signs for bad weather. They include:

- Increase in cloud cover and darkening skies
- Sudden decrease or increase in wind velocity
- Dramatic change in wind direction
- Lightning nearby or in the distance
- Thunder in the distance
- Gusty wind conditions.

A change in the weather can happen quickly. If there is any sign of bad weather, you should head for shore—pronto! Be conservative, and always watch for signs in the sky.

Bad Weather

Learn to identify the signs of good sailing weather and the warning signs of bad weather. At the first sign of threatening weather, head for shore—pronto! Changes in weather can happen quickly. Be conservative—if in doubt, don't go out!

Tides and Currents

TIDE TIPS:

Handy tide indicators include pilings on docks or the sand of the beach. If the sand or piling is dark and wet for a good portion above the water's edge, the tide is going out (receding). If the sand or piling is dry right to the water's edge, the tide is coming in (rising).

Understanding tide and current is just as important as understanding the wind. **Current** is the horizontal flow of water caused by tide or differences in elevation. **Tides** are the vertical movement of water caused by the gravitational pull of the moon on the earth. Tides occur daily at regular intervals. The difference between the height of water at low and high tide varies in different locations. Fresh water lakes usually do not have tides.

Both currents and tides are affected by water depth. Current will be stronger where water is deepest. You can determine the direction and speed of current by using certain handy **current indicators**. A floating object, such as a stick being carried along by the moving water, or water swirling past a fixed buoy or dock are good current indicators.

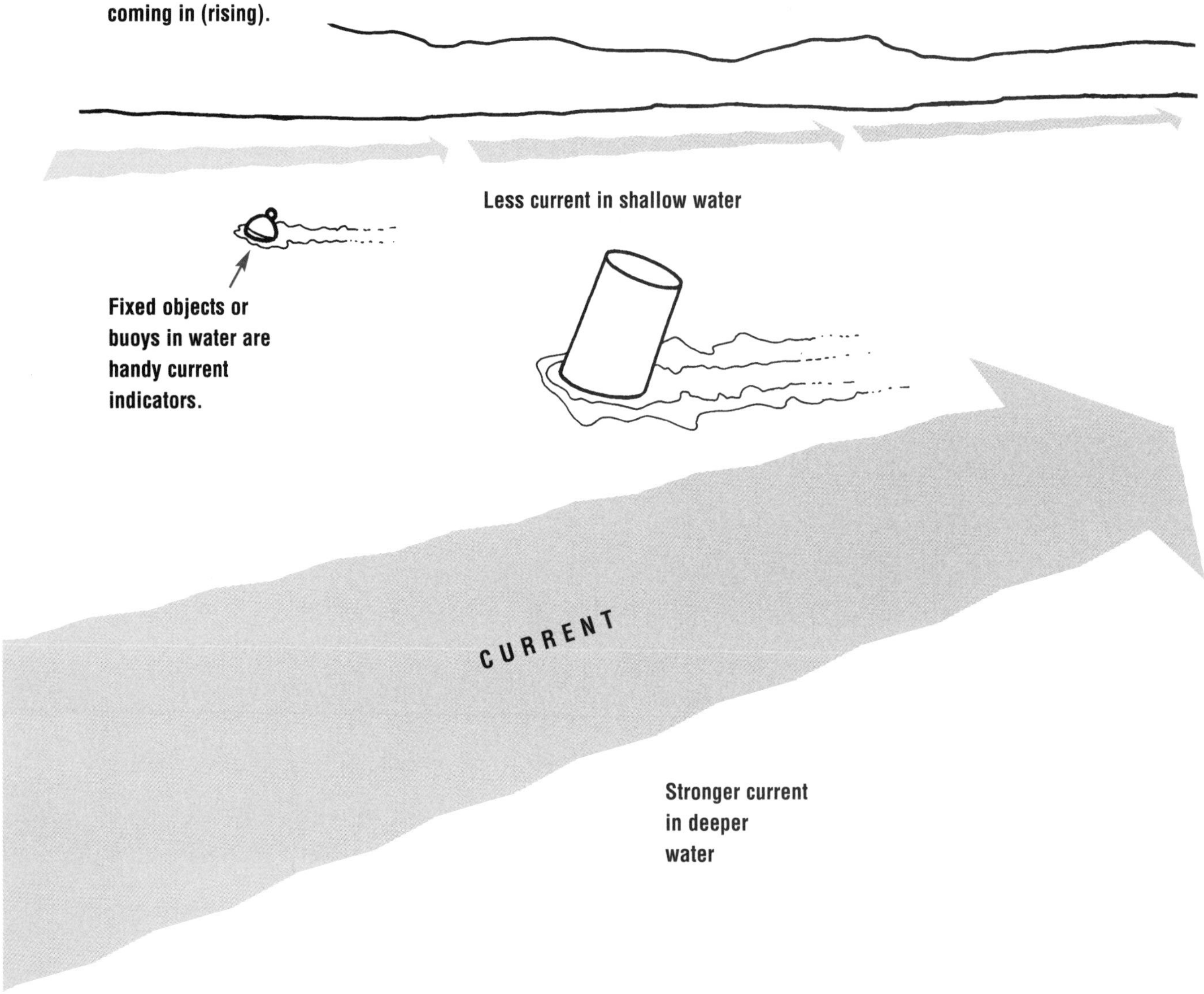

Less current in shallow water

Fixed objects or buoys in water are handy current indicators.

CURRENT

Stronger current in deeper water

Compensating for Current

An important part of your environmental awareness involves compensating for current. For instance, if the current is sweeping you to the right as you head back toward shore, you should correct by heading a bit to the left of your destination. If there is a fixed object (such as a buoy or moored boat) between you and the shore, you can use it as a reference by lining it up with another object on shore. If the two objects stay aligned, you are correctly compensating for current.

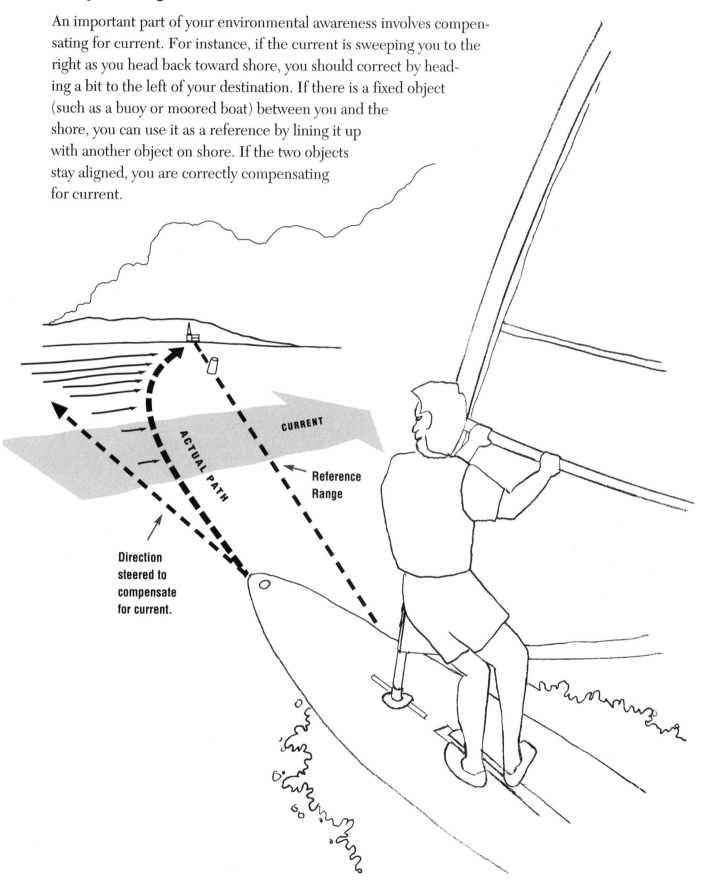

CURRENT

ACTUAL PATH

Reference Range

Direction steered to compensate for current.

14 *Beyond the Basics*

KEY CONCEPTS covered in this chapter:

- **Rig tuning**
- **Fine tuning (RAF-CAMBER)**
- **Railing and trimming**
- **Wetsuits and drysuits**
- **Harness**
- **Expanding your horizons**

As you gain more experience and log more time on your board, you will start getting into some of the finer points of windsurfing. For example, tuning your sail for maximum performance, controlling

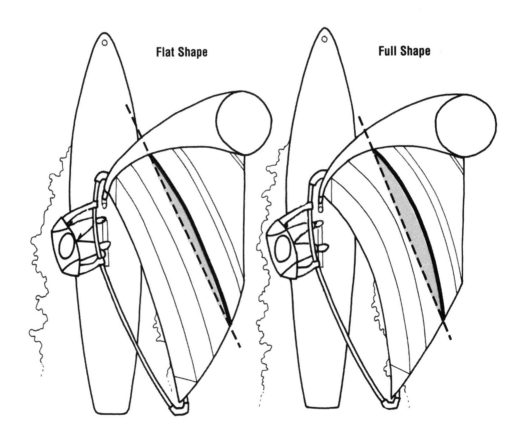

Flat Shape   Full Shape

your long or short board when it planes, and purchasing new gear and accessories for extending your range of conditions and fun.

The first thing to become more aware of is tuning your sail. The rigging instruction in the manual and what you learned from your instructor was just to get you started with a flat easy-to-use sail.

Fine Tuning

A full-battened sail has battens that run from the leech (back) all the way to the mast (front). Tuning the sail starts with the downhaul. While looking at the batten just above the boom, start downhauling. When this batten is just below the mast, your power to control is ideal. The top batten should be behind the mast and the leech is loose or dropping. Without enough downhaul the batten above the boom pokes out the front of the mast, the top batten is below the mast and the leech is tight. If the sail is rigged this way, it will have incredible power, but will be hard to control in strong wind. Too much downhaul and all of the battens are behind the mast, the leech is loose down to the booms, and the sail is completely flat even when full of wind. The sail has no power in this state, however, it is easy to control when the wind is strong.

The outhaul adjustment is now important once your downhaul is set. Pulling an inch or two of outhaul is usually ideal. Less outhaul gives you more power, more outhaul gives you less power.

A camber induced sail has a piece of plastic of some type, that sits between the batten and the mast, inside the luff sock. It creates draft (camber) in the sail even without any wind. As a plus, the cambered sail is faster, more stable, and can be used in a larger range of conditions. A minus is, it is heavier, usually has a bigger luff sleeve, harder to clear on water starts, and is more expensive. Cambered sails are tuned very similar to fully battened sails. We, however, pay more attention to the top batten and the leech looseness. The ideal downhaul tension has the first and second battens, from the top, behind the mast. The leech is loose on the third batten, or is at least dropped down from the mast. Just like the fully battened sail, more downhaul is less power and increased stability, and less downhaul is more power and less stability. Adjusting the outhaul will also change the power in the cambered sail and can help with points of sail performance. The ideal setting

Helpful Rigging Hints

- Try not to leave gaps between outhaul and downhaul cleats.

- Always tie off loose lines around the boom or base

- Mark your extensions and boom, or sails with setting information to speed up rigging.

- Rig cambered sails with the cambers pointing up.

- Pull only on the camber when threading through the mast.

is normally just an inch of pull on the outhaul. Without any outhaul tension (neutral outhaul) the sail has more power. Negative outhaul setting (boom shorter than the clew of the sail) creates even more power yet, also great for sailing downwind. A negative outhaul setting can be hard to control when overpowered.

Outhauling more than an inch (positive outhaul) will depower the sail and can help you with sailing (pointing) into the wind higher.

Sail Shape

Sail shape is adjusted by altering the **draft**, or curvature in a sail. Draft is controlled by adjusting vertical and horizontal tension on the sail with the downhaul and outhaul. The downhaul controls fore and aft as well as top to bottom location of the draft. The outhaul basically controls the depth of the draft.

Basically, a fuller, deeper sail produces more power while a flatter sail has less power. For a flatter sail, tighten both the outhaul and the downhaul. If there are wrinkles running horizontally across the sail,

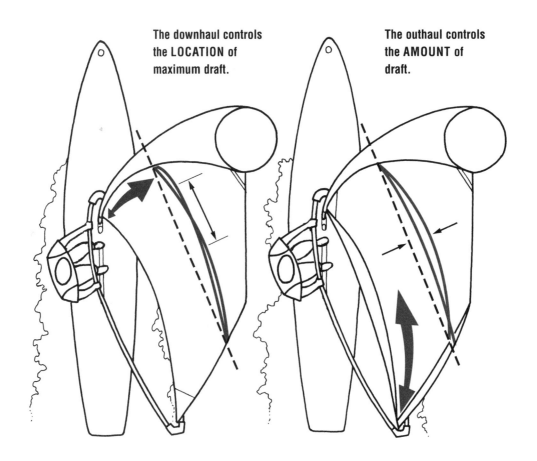

The downhaul controls the LOCATION of maximum draft.

The outhaul controls the AMOUNT of draft.

tighten the downhaul. If the wrinkles run up and down, parallel with the mast, tighten the outhaul. Never allow the sail to be so full that it touches the boom while powered-up.

Railing

As your skills improve and you find yourself handling stronger breezes, you will encounter a windsurfing phenomenon called **railing**. Railing occurs when the underwater lift from the centerboard causes the board to become unstable and roll from one side to the other. It only happens when the winds are strong enough for the board to accelerate and rise up (**plane**) on top of the water. You can stop the board's tendency to rail by simply retracting the centerboard slightly or opening the sail ("door") a little to reduce power. Some racing sailors intentionally rail their boards to get more speed because it reduces the wetted surface, hence drag. They also move their feet out on the rails and footstraps which greatly increases speed. But this technique requires experience. At this stage, keep the board flat on the surface

NOTE   Wide or shortboard beginner planing problems: With the centerboard fully retracted, or when learning on the wide-style shortboard (no centerboard) control while planing becomes easier (no centerboard lift). If you do experience control loss (the board bounces and weaves) while planing, extend your arms, straighten your legs, and lean your body out over the water farther. Your body will create lateral pressure against the fin, smoothing the board out at the same time taking your weight off the board allowing it to remain on a plane.

Railing

Railing can occur at high speeds when the lift from the centerboard causes the board to become unstable and roll from side to side. You can counteract railing by depowering the sail or retracting the centerboard slightly.

Clothing

Once you have mastered the basics and decided to make windsurfing one of your leisure time activities, you will want to add to your wardrobe.

To properly protect yourself against the cold, you will need a wetsuit or drysuit, and probably a cap and gloves. These effectively extend the sailing season in milder regions of the country, and make sailing in colder regions safer and more comfortable, whether it's mid-summer or late autumn.

Wetsuits

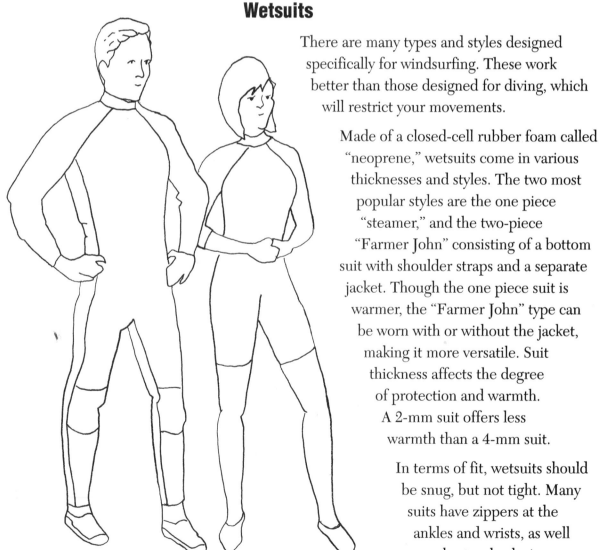

There are many types and styles designed specifically for windsurfing. These work better than those designed for diving, which will restrict your movements.

Made of a closed-cell rubber foam called "neoprene," wetsuits come in various thicknesses and styles. The two most popular styles are the one piece "steamer," and the two-piece "Farmer John" consisting of a bottom suit with shoulder straps and a separate jacket. Though the one piece suit is warmer, the "Farmer John" type can be worn with or without the jacket, making it more versatile. Suit thickness affects the degree of protection and warmth. A 2-mm suit offers less warmth than a 4-mm suit.

In terms of fit, wetsuits should be snug, but not tight. Many suits have zippers at the ankles and wrists, as well as chest or back zippers, which make them

One-piece and two piece wetsuits

easier to put on and take off. The zippers should open gradually, not burst open from the pressure of a too tight fit.

Wetsuits that are double-lined with nylon covering on the inside and outside are more durable and hard-wearing than single-lined suits with nylon only on the inside, but single-lined suits are more efficient in protection against cold.

Drysuits

Drysuits keep you warm by keeping water out. They are sealed at the neck, ankles, and wrists and are best for those who sail regularly in cold regions. If worn in warmer conditions, they are hot and sweaty. The modern windsurfing drysuit is similar to a wetsuit, except for the seals. It is made of neoprene and can be a one-piece suit with a full-length zipper across the shoulders, or a two-piece suit. Loose fabric type suits, which are popular with dinghy and big boat sailors and require thermal clothing underneath, are not suitable for windsurfing.

Gloves

Gloves do not work well for windsurfing. But if you sail in cold conditions or your hands get tender, there are special reinforced neoprene gloves for cold weather, and lightweight sailing gloves or garden gloves can be used for hand protection.

Drysuits

Drysuits are best for cold regions. They are sealed at the neck, wrists and ankles to keep water out.

Gloves

Special sailing gloves can help prevent sore hands, but can limit dexterity. For that reason, many are cut to leave fingertips exposed.

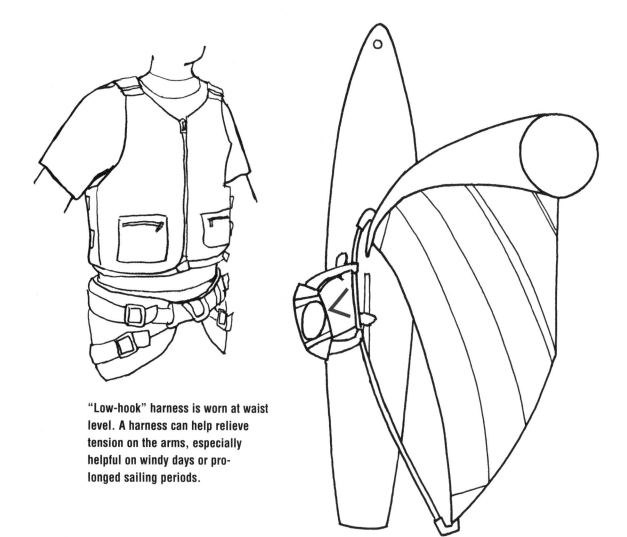

"Low-hook" harness is worn at waist level. A harness can help relieve tension on the arms, especially helpful on windy days or prolonged sailing periods.

Harness

A harness has a hook on the front that attaches to a line on the boom to relieve tension on the arms. Harnesses are worn in stronger winds to conserve energy and thereby extend time on the water. Intermediate experience is needed before attempting to use a harness. The most efficient harnesses are the "low hook" variety.

Expanding Your Horizons

One of the best things about the sport of windsurfing is its tremendous versatility. It means that even the most accomplished sailor will never get bored.

For those who want to expand their horizons, the choices include one-design racing, funboard racing (course and slalom), surfsailing, wave jumping, and freestyle. Each of these "disciplines" has unique challenges to be mastered. Exploring all the possibilities would more than fill a lifetime!

Because windsurfing gear is so portable, there's really no excuse for not finding a place that's just right for your "discipline" or skill level. If conditions at your local beach aren't suitable, pack up and hit the road!

A great way to advance your skill level fast is to take your next vacation at a spot where windsurfing and/or a windsurfing school are available. You can learn more in a week of concentrated sailing with good coaching than you would in a whole season on your own.

Michael Gebhart, Olympic Bronze Medalist in 1988 and Silver Medalist in 1992 in the Men's Mistral, awards medals to Junior Olympic sailors.

The fundamental skills discussed in this book and taught by US SAILING Certified Instructors will enable you to enjoy the sport of windsurfing for years to come. Using this solid, safe foundation, you can develop your skills to any level you desire — even the Olympics or Pro World Cup, if that's your dream.

The sky's the limit ... **DO IT!**

Appendix

Certificate Records

Part 1: Minimum Water Skills

The following skills are to be tested on the water for mastery. It is recommended that the chronological order of skills be followed as listed. To attain the mastery level, the student should be able to perform the skills safely and generally mistake free—judged on a basis that is appropriate for a learn-to-sail student. Criteria used for evaluation should include steering technique, sail trim, stance and grip, board handling skills, and student confidence. Falling or dropping the rig should not, on its own, be used as a criterion for not mastering a skill.

Student performance may be influenced by wind speed and direction, water conditions and air temperature. Recommended wind range for testing skills is three-to-six knots. Regional differences in typical conditions may require that this recommended wind range be modified.

1. **Rig a Board:** from components, then launch without assistance.

2. **Uphaul the Rig:** from downwind and from upwind to basic position.

3. **Maintain Basic Position**

4. **Turn Board:** from basic position, turn board in opposite direction (180 degrees) through no-go zone.

5. **Go to Sailing Position:** from basic position to sailing position.

6. **Sailing Position:** stance, grip, sail positions for different points of sail.

7. **Fail-safe Maneuver**

8. **Stopping Maneuvers:** slow and quick controlled stops.

9. **De-Rig to Self-Rescue:** de-rig to self-rescue position and paddle 100 yards.

10. **Rig from Self-Rescue:** from self-rescue position to sailing position.

11. **Tacking:** from reach to reach, closed-hauled to close-hauled.

12. **Jibing:** reach to reach, run to reach.

13. **Sailing a Rectangular Course**

14. **Landing without Assistance**

15. **De-Rig for Storage**

Part 2: Minimum Knowledge Skills

In addition to mastering the minimum water skills, a student is expected to be familiar with the following knowledge areas: right-of-way, safety, rig parts, board parts, points of sail, hypothermia, heat emergencies, weather, currents and tides. To successfully complete the requirements for a basic windsurfing certificate, you must answer 80% of the questions correctly on the knowledge test that your instructor will give you.

To prepare for your test, complete the following sample. If you score 80% (32 of 40) or more and review any questions you answered incorrectly, you should be ready for the knowledge test.

I. Multiple Choice – *Choose the best answer*

1. Before a person can take a US SAILING Level 1 Windsurfing Course, he or she must
   a) know the nautical terms.
   b) be able to swim.
   c) have previous sailing experience.
   d) be physically strong.

2. When rigging the sail, the first line to be fitted and tensioned is
   a) the outhaul.
   b) the uphaul.
   c) the inhaul.
   d) the downhaul.

3. A sailor de-rigs to self-rescue when
   a) he or she can paddle to shore.
   b) tired.
   c) he or she wants to.
   d) there is a cross-shore breeze.

4. A sailor should always climb onto the board from
   a) the downwind side.
   b) the upwind side.
   c) the side opposite the sail.
   d) the bow.

5. When uphauling from upwind and the rig and board starts to turn, you should
   a) move the front foot.
   b) stand firm.
   c) move any foot.
   d) move the back foot.

6. The rig is easiest to uphaul when the mast is lying
   a) towards the stern.
   b) towards the bow.
   c) on the downwind side.
   d) on the upwind side.

7. The basic position is a good position to use if
    a) you are unsure of what to do next.
    b) you want to turn around.
    c) you want to check the wind direction.
    d) all of the above.

8. When in the sailing position, the position of the feet should be
    a) front foot pointed forward, well behind the mast, and back foot is shoulder-width away and across the centerline, toe slightly forward.
    b) front foot pointed forward, in front of mast, and back foot across centerline on centerboard well.
    c) both feet pointed across board.
    d) both feet pointed across board with front foot behind mast and back foot next to front foot.

9. Moving the sail toward the back of the board makes
    a) the front of the board turn away from the wind.
    b) the front of the board turn toward the wind.
    c) the board jibe.
    d) the board fail-safe.

10. The best way to determine wind direction is
    a) put the rig in the basic position.
    b) put the rig in the sailing position.
    c) observe the drifting movement of the board.
    d) get a weather report.

11. When a puff starts to overpower the rig, you should first
    a) drop the rig.
    b) stand firm.
    c) close the sail.
    d) open the sail.

12. The fail-safe maneuver gets rid of power in your sail by
    a) dropping the rig in the water.
    b) leaning back to counterbalance the power.
    c) releasing the boom with your back hand and straighten your front arm.
    d) rolling up your sail.

13. Sailors should know the following visual signals:
    a) There is deep water here.
    b) I require assistance.
    c) I have right-of-way.
    d) Good surf.

14. You can get hypothermia by
    a) spending a lot of time in 75 degree F water.
    b) not wearing proper clothing.
    c) lowering your body temperature below 98.6 degrees F.
    d) all of the above.

15. A low pressure system usually means
    a) wind and rain.
    b) sunny weather and sea breezes.
    c) colder air and rain.
    d) strong sea breezes.

16. The ideal wind for windsurfing is
    a) offshore wind.
    b) onshore wind.
    c) cross-shore wind.
    d) sea breeze.

17. The direction of current can be determined by
    a) puffs and lulls on the water surface.
    b) small eddies and ripples around fixed objects in the water.
    c) gravitational moon charts.
    d) the direction the fish are swimming.

18. A port tack board should stay clear of
    a) a canoe.
    b) an oil tanker.
    c) a starboard tack board.
    d) all of the above.

II. Definitions (*in your own words briefly describe the following*)

19. Safety code (*list items*) _____

20. No-go zone _____

21. Onshore wind _____

22. Cross-shore wind _____

23. Offshore wind _____

III. Board and Sail Identification (*name and label points*)

25. A _____ 26. B _____ 27. C _____ 28. D

29. E _____ 30. F _____ 31. G _____ 32. H

IV. Points of Sail

33. I _____ 34. J _____ 35. K _____

36. L _____ 37. M _____

V. Right-of-Way (*Who has the right-of-way?*)

38. _____ 39. _____ 40. _____

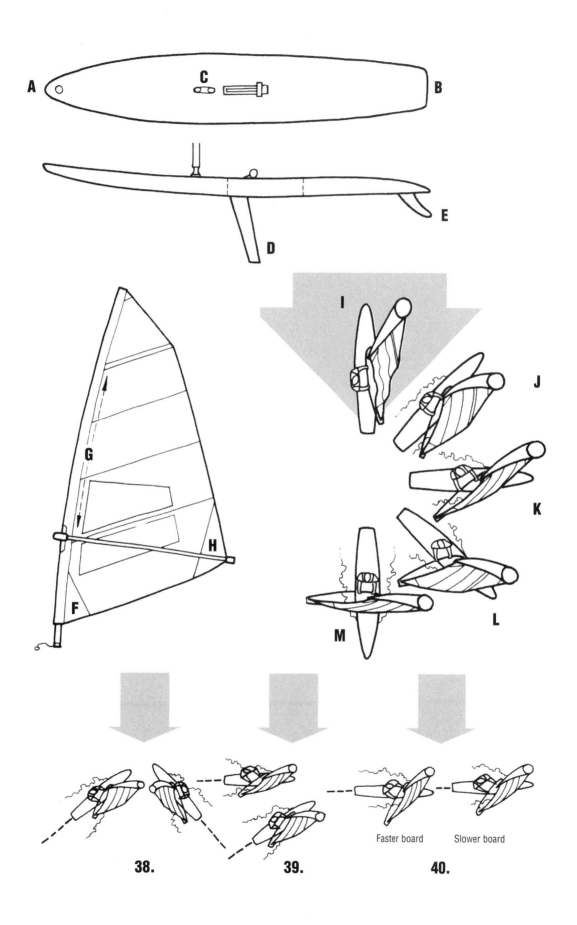

Faster board   Slower board

38.   **39.**   **40.**

Course Evaluation

Dear Student:

US SAILING needs your input to help make their courses the best possible for you and future students. Please fill out this form, and give it to your instructor, or mail it to:

US SAILING / Training Office
15 Maritime Drive, P.O. Box 1260
Portsmouth, RI 02871

Thanks for your help!

☐ MALE
☐ FEMALE

NAME   EMAIL   DATE OF BIRTH

ADDRESS   CITY   STATE   ZIP

LOCATION OF COURSE   INSTRUCTOR'S NAME

- Please use the scale below to rate this course:

Facilities	☐ poor	☐ fair	☐ good	☐ excellent
Condition of Boards	☐ poor	☐ fair	☐ good	☐ excellent
Textbooks	☐ poor	☐ fair	☐ good	☐ excellent
Instructors	☐ poor	☐ fair	☐ good	☐ excellent
Emphasis on Safety	☐ poor	☐ fair	☐ good	☐ excellent
Overall Course Rating	☐ poor	☐ fair	☐ good	☐ excellent

- If you could make one change to improve the quality of the course, what would it be?

- Was this course fun?   ☐ Yes ☐ No

- Would you recommend this course to friends?   ☐ Yes ☐ No

- What is your primary sailing interest after completing this course?
  - ☐ Recreational sailing
  - ☐ One-design racing
  - ☐ Funboard sailing
  - ☐ Funboard racing
  - ☐ Freestyle
  - ☐ Surfsailing
  - ☐ Instructing

Membership Applications

United States Sailing Association

Congratulations on completing the best instructor certification course in the country. As you begin sailing on your own, you may want to join America's foremost family of sailors, and enjoy travel savings, discounts on the best sailing books and videos, a free racing rulebook and more! As the national governing body for the sport of sailing, US SAILING has been serving the needs of sailors since 1897. Headquartered in Rhode Island, we are a non-profit organization involved in, and your advocate for, every aspect of the sport. We are the organization that binds together sailors, clubs, classes, fleets, and associations to create one source that every sailor can turn to for education, administration, advocacy and leadership.

US SAILING Individual Membership:

☐ $60.00 for 1 year ☐ $110.00 for 2 years ☐ $145.00 for 3 years
☐ $25.00 Youth (under 21 or full-time student)

Please make checks payable to US SAILING, and return along with this application to:

US SAILING / Membership Department, 15 Maritime Drive, P.O. Box 1260, Portsmouth, RI 02871

NAME _____ EMAIL _____ HOME PHONE _____ BUSINESS PHONE _____

ADDRESS _____ CITY _____ STATE _____ ZIP _____

CHECK ONE: ☐ VISA ☐ MC ☐ AMEX   NAME ON CREDIT CARD _____ CARD NUMBER _____ EXPIRATION DATE _____

US Windsurfing Association

info@uswindsurfing.org
To join and for more information, please visit **www.uswindsurfing.org**

US Windsurfing Membership:

☐ Individual: $35.00   ☐ Family: $45.00   ☐ Junior (under 19): $15.00

Selecting Equipment

Selecting Your Board

Once you have completed your course and received your US SAILING windsurfing instructor certification card, you may want to buy a board. Since there are so many different types, sizes, and manufacturers, you will need to make two basic decisions before starting your search.

- **How much do you want to spend?**

- **What are the average conditions for your area?** Are they light or windy, flat or choppy?

If there is a beach or a launching site nearby that is used by the local sailors, stop by and get their input on conditions and equipment. There may be a local windsurfing club, association or just an informal group of enthusiasts who meet regularly in your area. They will be more than happy to talk with you about board, rig, and sail types most suitable for you. Visit your local windsurfing store. If the attendants windsurf, they can provide good advice.

With your budget and design guidelines established, you can start your search. You will find that boards are divided into two categories. Longboard (with centerboard) and shortboard. In each class of board there are many differences. Boards are divided by length, width, volume, construction, and shape (outline, rocker, rail shape, bottom shape). For now, we will just look at construction and volume. As a beginner, you are looking toward a high volume board exceeding 200 liters.

Board Construction

Boards are built with a foam core inside either a plastic or resin based shell. Common plastic based materials are polyethelene and ASA. These are generally less expensive, more durable and heavier than polyester, epoxy resin or carbon fiber composites used on more sophisticated boards.

Weight is also worth considering if you have to lift the board on and off the roof of your car and carry it to the water every time you sail. The lighter and more rigid a board is, the more fragile and expensive it will be. However, board design and construction have improved so much in recent years that the modern production board is stronger, lighter, and faster than a custom board built five years ago.

There are several methods of construction used by manufacturers.

- **Blow molding construction** is popular among builders of production boards at the lower end of the price scale. This process involves using intense pressure to force hot polyethelene inside a mold, which is then filled with foam.

- **ASA construction** involves molding the board shell in two halves—a top and a bottom. The critical part in this process is the method by which the two halves are joined before being filled with foam.

- **Composite construction** represents the state of the art in board construction. A lightweight foam core blank is covered with layers of high-tech fibers, generally glass and carbon, bonded with resin.

Types of Boards

Recreational Board

One-Design / Racing Board

Recreational Board / Beginner Board

Short Board

Equipment – Island Sports, Middletown, Rhode Island

The ideal skin material for a recreational board is the ASA-type plastic because of its greater durability, impact resistance, ease of repair, and waterproof consistency. Polyethelene is favored for school and rental use because it is very resilient; but it is heavier than the other materials. Composite boards offer the lightest weight, and best strength to weight ratio, but are at the higher end of the price range and are fragile.

Board Volume

A very important consideration when looking at a board is its amount of flotation. A board's volume is a measure of its flotation—and the greater the volume, the greater the flotation. Volume is usually described in units of liters. Heavy-weight people need more volume to support their weight than do lighter people or children. Shorter, lower volume boards move faster than longer, higher volume boards, but they require more wind and skill to sail. For the new sailor, a board with 220-to-260 liters of volume will be stable and easy-to-handle. Standard training boards used by schools are in this range.

Board Shape

The board that you learned on was probably a school or all-round recreational type with a wide stern and flat bottom. These features produce a stable board that is easy to sail in light winds and forgiving in terms of handling. It is a good recreational board for light-to-moderate winds, which can be enjoyed for many years.

Board Categories

- **Recreational (beginner) longboards** are between 3.07 meters (10'0") to 381 meters (12'6") in length and ranging in volume from 210 liters to 260 liters. They are designed for stability and ease of maneuvering. Recreational longboards have adjustable mast tracks or footstraps. Recreational boards are durable, inexpensive and can be a little heavy.

- **Course racing longboards** are similar in length and volume to the recreational longboard. These boards are designed to sail upwind and have long adjustable mast tracks, footstraps, and large centerboards. Course racing longboards are lightweight fast hulls and can be sailed in almost all conditions. Unfortunately, they can be expensive in cost.

- **One-design boards** range from 3.61 meters (11'10") to 3.81 meters (12'6") long with 195 to 250 liters of volume, and are designed for maximum pointing ability and high speeds both on and off the wind without being extreme in design. They offer good all-round performance in virtually any wind condition. Large manufacturers each have their own brand of "one-design."

- **Shortboards** do not have a centerboard, although they may have a small center fin to help with upwind sailing when non-planing. Shortboards come in many shapes and sizes, but are generally shorter than 3.07 meters (10'). Course racing, formula, and beginner shortboards are very wide (70 cm and up) packing lots of volume (150 liters or more). The race versions have footstraps out on the edge of the board. These boards are generally very light, expensive and fragile. The beginner widestyle shortboard is stable, has positions available for the footstraps closer to the centerline, reasonably priced and maneuverable. The smaller shortboards can be designed for speed as in a slalom board. The bump and jump and free ride boards are designed for maneuverability and wave boards are designed for the waves.

Selecting Your Board: Selection of Mast, Boom, and Sail

When you buy your first board, it will usually come as a complete package with mast, boom, and sail included. Later on, when you become an experienced sailor, you may want to select a mast, boom, and sail suitable for your particular style.

- **Mast** The mast should be strong and light. In addition, it must be matched to the sail in its bend characteristics. Select a stiff boom that has strong end fittings and an efficient clamp system.

- **Sails** If you can afford it, buy two sails. Depending on the prevailing wind conditions in your area, a good combination could be a 5.0 and a 6.3 square meter sail, which represent a medium-small and medium-size sail. Generally, the lighter the wind, the larger the sail has to be to generate more power. Medium-small sails are best for strong winds and novice sailors. In the beginning, you will use the medium-small sail to develop your basic board handling skills, and as your skills improve you will switch to the bigger sail and reserve the smaller sail for its designed purpose—strong winds.

Types of Sails

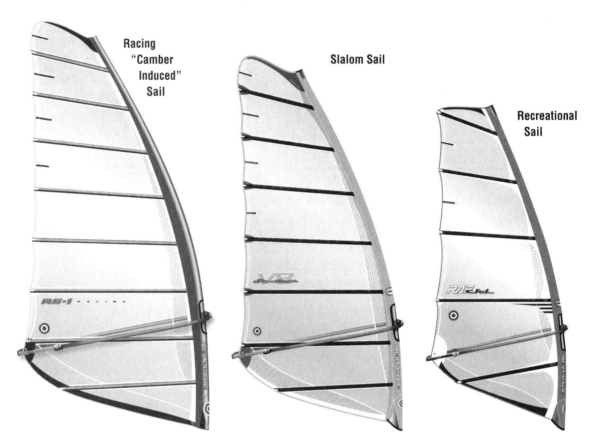

Racing "Camber Induced" Sail

Slalom Sail

Recreational Sail

© NeilPydre

If you plan to use different size sails, look for packages that include a mast extension unit and buy only adjustable booms to accommodate the difference sizes.

Sails are made of dacron, mylar, or mono-film. Dacron is least expensive, fairly durable and easy to maintain. However, it stretches and can lose its shape after a period of use. Mylar is more expensive, stronger and less stretchy. Mono-film is also inexpensive, lightweight, impact resistant, but will tear to the seams if ripped and will not stretch. The more battens, cambers, thickness of film, graphics, and the bigger the sail, the more expensive.

Keep your rig simple to maximize your knowledge and enjoyment. It would be wise to wait until you can really handle your board and big sail before getting into hi-tech equipment. As your skills improve, you will be in a position to better appreciate the difference that the more sophisticated equipment can make to your performance.

Preventative Maintenance

To get the most out of your equipment – take care of it. The most common cause for damage or failure to your equipment is sand and salt water. When you get back to shore or home, hose down your board, mast, boom, and sail, making sure to rinse out the centerboard well, mast track, universal joint and boom extensions. Get in the habit of systematically checking your equipment before and after you go sailing. Here's a basic checklist:

- Pop rivets on boom and mast extension
- Mast foot and universal joint
- All lines and cleats
- Safety leash
- Sail, including seams, grommets (eyes) in the tack and clew, any batten pockets, and reinforcement at top of sleeve
- Skeg and attachment screws or bolts
- Centerboard (or daggerboard) and centerboard well for fit and movement

Basic Board Repairs

Unless you have experience in working with resins and plastics, you should attempt repairs to only minor scrapes, dents or "dings." Two-part epoxy fillers, such as Marine-tex or inexpensive epoxy fillers used for body work on cars, are ideal for this type of damage, followed by sanding (with a block), polishing, and buffing. Some plastic adhesives and fillers will have an adverse reaction with certain foam cores used inside the board. Consult your local board shop and follow the manufacturer's instructions regarding repair materials.

Cosmetic blemishes and fine scratches can be removed by using fine grit wet and dry sandpaper (starting with 400 and finishing with 600) and/or a polishing compound. Automotive shops are a good source for polishing compounds and buffing pads.

Car-Topping

Because boards are lightweight, many sailors carry them on top of their cars. But there are right ways to car-top, and there are wrong ways. The proper techniques will avoid danger to other drivers, minimize wear on your equipment, as well as reduce windage, noise, vibration and fuel consumption.

There are two parts to car-topping right:

1) a good roof rack and tie-downs
2) proper positioning of the board and equipment

Roof Rack and Tie-Downs

The weight of a board, mast, boom and sail (45-60 pounds) combined with their considerable drag and lift puts a large load on any roof rack. It is important that the rack is strong and securely attached to the roof. Some racks that come with the car from the factory are not suitable for this.

There are roof racks specifically designed for transporting boards that use a system of brackets and clips to secure the equipment to the rack and the rack to the roof. Some of them also have anti-theft locks so you don't have to worry about leaving your board on the car.

Use buckle-type straps instead of rope to secure your board and equipment. You will find straps are easier and quicker to fasten than rope—and you don't have to worry about tying hitches that may slip or get jammed. There is also a strap system that uses clips on one side of the rack and a ratchet winding device on the other end for tightening the straps. Shock cord is not a secure way of fastening your board to the rack.

Beware of accumulative sun damage on your straps. One season of riding around on top of your car and your straps may become greatly weakened by UV rays. Be sure and monitor their deterioration. Never use bungie cord to tie boards to racks.

If your rack doesn't have any padding, you can use sponges, specially made foam rack pads, or foam packing material to protect your equipment. Most board shops can fix you up with specially shaped packing inserts.

Positioning the Equipment

Mercedes Benz conducted wind tunnel tests on boards carried on roof racks, and the findings showed that wind noise and drag could be reduced by positioning the equipment in the following manner:

1. The bow of the board should point toward the front of the car.

2. The top surface (deck) of the board should be facing downward with the skeg pointing upward.

3. The overhang at the front of the car should be as little as possible—just enough to balance the board before securing.

Wind tunnel tests conducted by Mercedes Benz have established the importance of proper board positioning when car topping.

Some more tips:

4. If two boards are carried on the same rack, they should be one on top of the other, pointing toward the front of the car, with foam padding between to eliminate damaging chafe.

5. Never tie down booms or masts on top of a hull. The vibration can cause dents in the board's skin and possible delamination of the skin from the foam core.

6. Carry booms and masts alongside the hulls. Another efficient, but rarely used method is to sling the boom and mast under the rack. Use this method only if the rack is padded.

7. Always remove the centerboard, mast foot, or any other small, detachable fittings before car topping.

Be aware:

Car-topped gear collects lots of dust and road grime which will affect the anti-skid surface of the board. A soft-scrub cleaner (use sparingly) is an excellent means to revitalize the original condition. Better yet is to use board and gear covers whenever you cartop.

A full-length mast will project well behind the back of the car, so be sure to tie a red flag or red cloth on the end of the mast to warn pedestrians and following traffic.

Drills for Improving Technique

When you go out to practice and perfect your skills, it is helpful to use a mark or marks to sail around. It is much easier to measure your progress executing maneuvers within a measured distance. An empty plastic water jug or plastic bleach bottle with a small weight and lightweight anchor line will serve well as a mark and is inexpensive to make. They are also easy to carry and launch from your board. Start with simple drills which involve tacking and jibing. It is more beneficial to perform multiple repetitions of maneuvers than just sail long straight line reaches.

Below are some suggestions for practice courses.

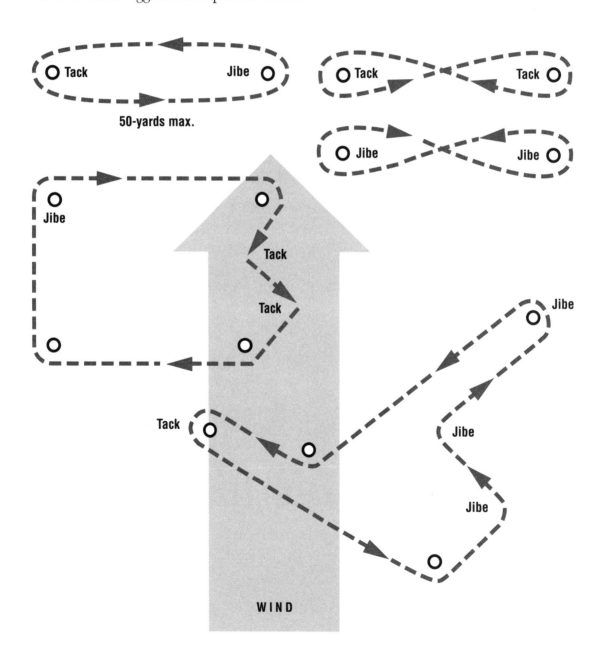

Information

- For information concerning basic windsurfing, intermediate and racing courses, instructional manuals, and certified instructors:

  US SAILING 401 683-0800

  P.O. Box 1260, Portsmouth, RI 02871

  windsurfing@ussailing.org

  www.ussailing.org

- For information concerning basic sailing, canoeing, kayaking, swimming, lifeguarding, first aid, CPR, instructional manuals, videos and certificates:

  American Red Cross 202 737-8300

  National Headquarters, 17th and D Streets NW, Washington, DC 20006

  www.redcross.org

- For information concerning recreational and racing events, clubs, water access and safety:

  US Windsurfing 877 386-8708

  421 79th Avenue, St. Pete Beach, FL 33706

  info@uswindsurfing.org

  www.uswindsurfing.org

- For information concerning the business end of teaching or running a windsurfing school, including marketing tips, business plans, case studies, and applications for free marketing materials and co-op advertising support:

  AWIA – American Windsurfing Industries Association 800 963-7873

  10.99 Snowden Road, White Salmon, WA 98672

  info@awia.org

  www.awia.org

- For information concerning national laws and regulations for water safety, boating and equipment requirements:

  U.S. Coast Guard Commandant 202 267-2229

  2100 2nd Street SW, Washington, DC 20593-0001

  www.uscg.mil

- For information concerning weather, water and charts:

  NOAA – National Oceanic & Atmospheric Administration 800 638-8972

  FAA Distribution Division, AVN-530, National Aeronautical Charting Office

  Riverdale, MD 20737-1199

  weather.noaa.gov

  iwin.nws.noaa.gov

Glossary of Sailing Terms

This glossary is a reference source for words and expressions used in this book as well as those frequently heard on the beach or on the water. Words having the same or similar meaning (synonyms) are also included to assist in word association and account for regional differences in the sailing language.

Abeam A direction off the side of a board, at right angles to a line from bow to stern.
Syn. On the beam.

Aerobic Exercises Activity such as bicycling, jogging, or swimming which stimulates the cardio-vascular system.

Aft 1. Towards, near, or at the back end of a board. *Syn.* Astern.
2. A direction behind the stern of a board. *Syn.* Astern.

Anaerobic Exercises Activity such as lifting weights which helps promote strength, flexibility, and muscle development.

Anemometer A device used to indicate wind speed.

Apparent Wind The wind that flows over a moving board, which is the combination of the "true wind" and "wind created" by the forward movement of the board.

Astern *See Aft.*

Athwartships A sideways direction on a board that is at a right angle to the line from bow to stern.

Barometer A device used to indicate atmospheric pressure.

Batten A strip or tube inserted into a pocket on the sail.

Beam The width of a board at its widest point.

Beam Reach Sailing at approximately 90 degrees to the wind source with the wind coming from abeam and the sail let out about half-way. (One of the points of sail.)

Bear Away *See Head Down.*

Bear Off *See Head Down.*

Beating Sailing toward the wind source, or against the wind, with the sail pulled in, tacking as you go, to reach a destination upwind.
Syn. Close Hauled, On the Wind, Sailing to Weather, Sailing to Windward, Sailing Upwind.

Block The nautical term for a pulley. It can have one or more sheaves, or wheels.

Boom A wishbone spar, joined at both ends, used to hold out the sail.

Bow The front (forward) end of a board.

Breeze Wind

Broad Reach Sailing with the wind coming over the rear corner of the board (with the bow approximately 135 degrees off the wind source. (One of the points of sail.)

By the Lee Sailing downwind with the wind blowing over the leeward side of the board, increasing the possibility of an unexpected jibe.

Centerboard A pivoting foil-shaped blade that projects below the bottom of a board to help prevent the board from sliding sideways.

Centerline An imaginary line that runs down the center of the board from the bow to the stern. *Syn*. Fore-and-aft line.

Cleat A plastic or metal-toothed device which is used to hold or secure lines.

Clew The lower back corner of the sail.

Close the Sail To pull in the boom and sail (to close the door). The opposite of "open the sail" (open the door). *Syn*. Sheet in.

Close-Hauled Describes a board sailing as close to the wind as possible with its sail pulled in. (One of the points of sail.) *Syn*. Beating, On the wind, Sailing to weather, Sailing to windward, sailing upwind.

Close Reach Sailing with the wind just forward of abeam, or with the bow approximately 70 degrees to the wind source. (One of the points of sail.)

Come About To turn the bow of a board through the wind, or no-go zone, so that the sail fills on the opposite side. *Syn*. tacking.

Come Down *See head down.*

Come Up *See head up.*

Coming About *See tack.*

Constant Angle to the Wind The correct angle of the sail to the wind, which remains the same when the sail is correctly trimmed (positioned) for all points of sail, except when the wind is blowing from behind the board.

Control Signals Hand signs used between instructors and students to communicate on the water.

Course The direction that a board is steered to reach a destination.

Current The movement of water caused by tides, wind, or change in elevation.

Daggerboard A vertically moving foil-shaped blade that is let down below the bottom of a board to help prevent the board from sliding sideways. Similar to the centerboard, except it is raised and lowered vertically rather than pivoted.

Deck The top surface of a board.

De-Rigging Undoing mast, boom, and sail and preparing them for storage or self-rescue.

Downhaul A line attached to the tack and the mast base fitting that adjusts the tension on the luff of the sail.

Downwind 1. Sailing away from the wind source with the sail let out. (One of the points of sail.) *Syn*. Run, With the wind.

2. In the opposite direction from the wind source, or where the wind is blowing to. *Syn.* Leeward.

Downwind Side *See Leeward side.*

Drogue The rig is used as a drogue, or sea anchor, by dragging it in the water to slow down the drifting movement in windy conditions.

Ease *See open the sail.*

Electrical Hazards Overhead power lines, electrical cables, electrical power tools and equipment used near the water, or near launching and board storage areas.

Environmental Awareness The continuous monitoring of wind, temperature, weather, sea conditions, current, and distance from the shore.

Fail-Safe A method of depowering the sail completely without dropping it in the water.

Fall Off *See head down.*

Feathering Sailing upwind so close to the wind that the forward edge of the sail is stalling or luffing, reducing the power generated by the sail. *Syn.* Light, Pinching, Sailing thin.

Foot The bottom edge of a sail, also a mast base

Fore Towards, near, or at the bow.

Fore and Aft Towards, near, or at both ends of a board. *Syn.* Front and back

Glide Zone The distance a board takes to coast to a stop after turning into the no-go zone or letting out its sail.

Go Up *See head up.*

Gust *See puff.*

Gybe *See jibe.*

Gybing *See jibing.*

Harden Up *See head up.*

Head The top corner of a sail.

Head Down To turn the board away from the wind.
    Syn. Bear away, Bear off, Come down, Fall off, Head off.

Head Off *See head down.*

Head Up To turn the board toward the wind. *Syn.* Bear up, Come up, Go up, Harden up, Luff up.

Heading The direction in which a board is pointing.

Head-to-Wind When the bow of a board is pointing directly into the wind, or in the middle of the no-go zone.

High Pressure Higher atmospheric pressure generally associated with fair skies and good weather.

Hole (in the Wind) *See lull.*

Hull Sailboard, excluding rig.

Hyperpyrexia Increase in body temperature caused by prolonged exposure to the sun, heat, and humidity. *Syn.* Heat Emergencies.

Hypothermia Reduction in body temperature caused by prolonged exposure to cold temperatures or cold water.

In the Groove When a board is moving well with proper balance and sail trim, and is steered so the sail is working at its best.

Jet Stream A snake-like river of air at about 35,000 feet in the atmosphere which affects the positions and movement of high and low pressure systems.

Jibe 1. To swing the sail across the front of the board when changing from one tack to the other when sailing downwind. *Syn.* Gybe.
2. The maneuver of changing from one tack to the other when sailing downwind.
Syn. Gybe, Jibing, Gybing.

Jibing 1. The maneuver of changing from one tack to the other when sailing downwind.
Syn. Gybing, Jibe, Gybe.

Jury Rig A temporary fix or replacement to damaged equipment which enables a board to be sailed.

Knot One nautical mile per hour. One knot equals 1.2 miles per hour.

Land Breeze *See offshore wind.*

Lee An area sheltered from the wind, such as a lee behind a wall, trees, or island.

Lee Shore The shore that is downwind of a board or boat.

Lee Side *See leeward side.*

Leech The back edge of a sail (between the head and clew).

Leeward In the opposite direction from the wind source; where the wind is blowing to.
Syn. Downwind.

Leeward Side The side of an object, such as a board, sail or land, that is away from the wind source.
Syn. Downwind side, Lee side, Low side.

Leeway The distance a board is pushed to leeward of its course by the action of the wind or current.

Lift 1. The aerodynamic or hydrodynamic force that results from air passing by a sail, or water flowing past a centerboard.
2. A change in wind direction which lets the board head up.

Light 1. When only the forward edge of a sail is stalling or luffing.
Syn. Feathering, High, Luffing, Pinching, Soft.
2. Description for low wind speed. *Syn.* Soft.

Line A rope used for a function on a board, i.e., downhaul, outhaul, uphaul, safety leash.

Low Pressure Lower atmospheric pressure generally associated with clouds, rain, and inclement weather.

Luff 1. The forward edge of a sail.
2. To stall or flap the sail at its forward edge, or over the entire sail.

Luff Up *See head up.*

Luffing When the sail is stalling or flapping at its forward edge, or the entire sail is flapping. *Syn.* Feathering, High, Light, Pinching, Soft.

Lull A decrease in wind speed for a short duration. *Syn.* Hole.

Mast A spar placed vertically on a board to hold up the sail.

Masthead The top of a mast.

Mooring A permanent anchor connected to a buoy by a rope and/or chain, to which a boat may be fastened.

No-Go Zone The area into the wind where no sailcraft can sail. The zone covers the direction pointing directly into the wind source and extending to about 45 degrees on either side of it.

Off the Wind Any of the points of sail, except close-hauled and no-go zone.

Offshore Away from the shore.

Offshore Wind Wind blowing away from the shore onto the water. *Syn.* Land Breeze.

One-Design Any board built to conform to rules so that it is identical to all others in the same class.

Onshore Toward the shore.

Onshore Wind Wind blowing from the water onto the shore. *Syn.* Sea Breeze.

On the Beam *See abeam.*

On the Wind *See upwind.*

Open the Sail To let out the boom and sail (to open the door). The opposite of "close the sail" (close the door). *Syn.* Ease, Let Off.

Outhaul A control line that is passed through the hole in the clew of the sail and attached to the back end of the boom

PFD A Personal Flotation Device. *Syn.* Life Jacket, Life Vest.

Pinching *See feathering.*

Planing When a board accelerates enough to break loose from its bow wave and ride on top of the water.

Points of Sail The headings of a board in relation to the wind, i.e., close-hauled, close reach, reach, broad reach, run, no-go zone.

Port The left side of a board when looking forward.

Puff A sudden increase in wind speed for a short duration.

Push-Pull Principle The way a sail generates power to propel a board through the water. The wind acts to push and/or pull the board.

Rake To lean the rig toward the bow or stern, sideways, or any other direction.

Reach Sailing with the board across or sideways to the wind. (One of the points of sail.)

Rig 1. The mast, mast foot, boom, and sail as a single unit.
2. To assemble the board, mast, mast foot, boom, and sail for sailing.

Right-of-Way A right-of-way board has precedence over others on conflicting courses and has the right to maintain its course.

"Rules of the Road" Laws establishing right-of-way in different situations that are intended to prevent collisions on the water.

Run Sailing away from the wind source with the sail let out and the wind coming over the back of the board. (One of the points of sail.) *Syn.* Downwind, With the wind.

Safety Leash A line, one end of which is attached to the rig and the other end to the board, that keeps the rig and board together when the mast foot is disconnected. *Syn.* Security line.

Sail Trim The positioning and shape of the sail to the wind. *Syn.* Set.

Sailor's Code Standards of behavior and courtesy demonstrated by sailors to other boaters.

Sea Breeze Wind blowing from the water toward the land resulting from the warm air rising over the land and drawing in the cooler air from the sea. *Syn.* Onshore wind.

Sea Conditions The size, shape, and frequency of the waves.

Security Line *See safety leash.*

Self Reliant The ability to sail and react to changing conditions by oneself without needing outside assistance.

Self-Rescue The maneuver of rolling up the sail to the mast, lashing the mast, sail, and boom together on top of the board, and paddling back to shore.

Set The direction in which current flows. *Syn.* Drift.

Soft *See light.*

Spar A pole used to support a sail, such as a mast or boom.

Squall A strong wind of short duration, usually appearing suddenly and accompanied by rain.

Starboard The right side of a board when looking forward.

Stern The back end of a board.

Tack 1. To turn the bow of a board through the wind or no-go zone so that the sail fills on the opposite side. *Syn.* Come About.
2. When the wind is blowing on a side of a board on any of the points of sail (does not include the no-go zone), i.e., starboard tack, port tack.
3. The forward lower corner of a sail.

Tacking The maneuver of turning a board through the no-go zone with the sail passing over the back of the board to change from one tack to the other when sailing upwind.
Syn. Come about.

Tidal Current The horizontal movement of water caused by tides.

Tide The vertical rise and fall of water caused by the gravitational forces of the moon and sun.

To Weather *See upwind.*

Tow Eye A small eye on the front of the board, used to attach a towline.

Trim To adjust a sail by moving the boom. *Syn.* Set.

True Wind The actual speed and direction of the wind felt when standing still.

Universal Joint A flexible or mechanical joint that allows the rig to move in any direction.

Upwind 1. Sailing toward the wind source, or against the wind, with the sail pulled in, tacking as you go. *Syn.* Beating, Close hauled, On the wind, Sailing to weather, Sailing to windward.
2. In the direction of the wind source or where the wind is blowing from.
Syn. Windward, To weather.

Upwind Side *See windward side*

Weather Shore The shore that is upwind of a board or boat.

Weather Side *See windward side.*

Wind Sensing Determining wind direction and velocity using feel, sight, and hearing.

Windward In the direction toward the wind source; where the wind is blowing from.
Syn. To weather, Upwind.

Windward Side The side of an object, such as a board, sail or land, that is toward the wind source. *Syn.* Weather side, Upwind side.

With the Wind *See run.*

Index

US SAILING
P.O. Box 1260, 15 Maritime Drive
Portsmouth, RI 02871

401 683-0800
Fax: 401 683-0840

info@ussailing.org
windsurfing@ussailing.org
www.ussailing.org